OUTSOU
AND THE VIRTUAL
ORGANIZATION

THE INCREDIBLE SHRINKING COMPANY

OUTSOURCING AND THE VIRTUAL ORGANIZATION

THE INCREDIBLE SHRINKING COMPANY

David Oates

CENTURY
BUSINESS

First published in 1998 by Century Ltd
Random House, 20 Vauxhall Bridge Road, London SW1V 2SA

Random House Australia (Pty) Limited
20 Alfred Street, Milsons Point
Sydney, New South Wales 2061, Australia

Random House New Zealand Limited
18 Poland Road, Glenfield
Auckland 10, New Zealand

Random House South Africa (Pty) Limited
Endulini, 5a Jubilee Road, Parktown 2193, South Africa

Random House UK Limited Reg. No. 954009

Papers used by Random House UK Limited are natural, recyclable
products made from wood grown in sustainable forests. The
manufacturing processes conform to the environmental
regulations of the country of origin.

ISBN 0 7126 7905 7

Companies, institutions and other organizations wishing to make
bulk purchases of any business books published by Random House
should contact their local bookstore or Random House direct:

Special Sales Director
Random House, 20 Vauxhall Bridge Road, London SW1V 2SA
Tel 0171 840 8470   Fax 0171 828 6681

www.randomhouse.co.uk
businessbooks@randomhouse.co.uk

Printed and bound in Great Britain by
Creative Print and Design Wales, Ebbw Vale

Contents

Foreword   vi

1. The Heart of the Matter   1

2. What is Outsourcing?   9

3. Core and Chore   27

4. Why Outsource?   41

5. The Mechanics of Outsourcing   65

6. Monitoring the Contract   99

7. The Benefits and Pitfalls of Outsourcing   113

8. Who Am I Working For?   135

9. The Virtual Organization – Myth or Reality?   163

Index   177

Foreword

After editing the international house magazine of a multinational industrial company for four years, I received the unwelcome news that it planned to contract out the responsibility for producing the magazine to an outside agency. Instead of working with three separate providers – editor, design house and printing firm – my client had decided that it would prefer to deal exclusively with a single agency that incorporated all three of these functions. The move would not only save money, it would take up far less of the client company's management time and allow it to concentrate on other more critical projects.

My first reaction was dismay. Although I was assured that my services would still be required (albeit as a feature writer rather than editor), I was confronted with the daunting prospect of having to forge new relationships with an organization I knew little about. I would have to re-negotiate the financial terms of a new working arrangement and it was clear from the start that these would be a lot less favourable than the existing contract. Probably worst of all, I was about to witness the disbandment of an editorial team that, after four years of trial and error, was beginning to work like a well-oiled machine.

The irony of all this was that I was in the middle of writing this book on outsourcing. I had virtually become a victim of the very subject I was researching. It rammed home to me something that had become increasingly evident from my researches – that outsourcing is steadily encroaching on all aspects of business life and that few people are likely to escape the consequences.

In fact, my circumstances were somewhat different from the average person who finds himself or herself subject to an outsourcing agreement. It normally happens to personnel who are on the permanent staff of the organization that has decided to contract out the running of a particular function. Legally, they are entitled to the same terms and conditions of employment when they transfer to the outsource provider as they are currently enjoying. In my case, as an independent homeworker (and, it could be argued, someone already performing an outsourced service) I could not expect such consolation benefits. I was back in the market place, having to negotiate terms and conditions with a new client.

On the other hand, I would not have to undergo the trauma of moving office from a familiar employer to one whose corporate ethos might be at variance with my existing circumstances. I was not left wondering whether I was about to be ejected from the cosiness of an organization I had grown comfortable with to one that might turn my world upside down.

Change for the better
All this sounds a little melodramatic and gives the impression that being outsourced is a curse worse than the black plague. As with most things, there is a reverse side to the coin that is more positive. Experience has shown that although most people faced with being outsourced initially view the prospect with some trepidation, it often proves to be a change for the better. People who might have felt that their careers were in the doldrums in

a small backwater of a major company suddenly find themselves working for an organization in which their expertise is highly valued and which offers far greater opportunities for advancement. Some people who have undergone precisely that experience tell their stories in case studies illustrated in this book.

It is the fear of the unknown that troubles most people caught up in the outsourcing trend. Once they have come to terms with the inevitable upheaval in their working lives, they often discover that it is the best thing that could have happened to them – but not everyone, of course. For some, it is not the specific work they do, but the organization they work for that motivates them. People in public service often do not relish being transferred to the cut and thrust of private enterprise, even if it does offer them a better chance for promotion. For the majority, however, if they recognize the advantages and seize the opportunities, being outsourced can provide a spirit of regeneration. It can give them the chance to re-invent themselves, to use a term that has become part of popular parlance.

For organizations which take the outsourcing route there are also pluses and minuses, as there are with any comparatively new management technique. For many companies outsourcing is coming to be regarded as a more humane and practical way to reduce overheads and focus on core activities than business process re-engineering (BPR), for example. For many, BPR has not delivered the goods and has resulted in the wholesale departure of too many talented employees. It is, of course, not the case that every outsourcing deal results in the staff involved being transferred to the service provider. In some cases, the provider can handle the project with its existing resources and that can be bad news for members of the staff of the outsourcing company, unless they can be redeployed to other parts of the organization (assuming they would want to be).

However, in many situations it is to everybody's advantage for the existing staff to stay with the work. It helps to achieve continuity and causes far less heartache. Fortunately, some of the leading outsource providers, such as Cap Gemini, are expanding so rapidly that they welcome waves of skilled employees joining their organization and offer excellent opportunities for such people to branch out into new areas.

For organizations contemplating the idea of outsourcing part of their operations, there are, of course, a lot of questions besides how to preserve the best interests of the departing workforce. They have to decide which functions are most appropriate for outsourcing. The simple solution is to keep core activities and outsource non-core. It is just a question of sifting core from chore. However, deciding which is which is not as easy as it sounds. This book is intended to help unravel such conundrums.

One thing is clear, however. As the benefits of outsourcing become increasingly apparent, organizations are becoming more and more adventurous in selecting the functions they feel confident about contracting out to an external provider. Initially, catering, cleaning services and property management were seen as the kind of safe functions to entrust to outside hands. Areas such as finance, human resources and legal services gave rise to concerns about security and confidentiality, as well as whether an outside service provider could ever be as knowledgeable about the internal workings of an organization as its in-house management.

Many of these concerns, however, have melted away, as outsourcing has encroached ever deeper into the core of organizations. There are few functions nowadays that are re-garded as sacrosanct, and nobody in any function can rest entirely easy in the sure knowledge that he or she operates in a safe haven. As the concept of the virtual organization starts to take hold, the prospect is held out of skeletal companies run by a handful of central office staff and where nearly all the functions previously run in-house have been farmed out to external specialists. This is good news for those who have joined the swelling ranks of independent specialists and service providers, but for company man, the person who prefers the apparent stability of corporate life, in a safe and secure job, the future is somewhat bleak.

Opinions differ on whether the virtual organization will ever become reality (if that doesn't sound like a contradiction in terms). However, there is little doubt that outsourcing has proved itself sufficiently successful to encourage organizations to look more closely at exactly what should be managed in-house and what should be contracted out. As the pressures increase on companies to cut costs and look for strategic advantage in an ever more competitive market place, it seems inevitable that outsourcing will become an increasingly popular bolt-hole.

1
The Heart of the Matter

Company diversification was all the rage in the 1960s and 1970s as companies tried to spread their options and to hedge their bets against downturns in their core activities. However, in the 1980s the pendulum swung in the opposite direction. Diversification went out of favour. It was seen as spreading resources too thinly. Popular wisdom was that it was best to concentrate on core activities where companies had long-established experience and had built up a body of expertise. This trend was accentuated during the recession of the late 1980s and early 1990s. Organizations' knee-jerk reaction was to cut costs. One of the immediate ways to do this was to withdraw into the corporate shell and pull all the operations in-house, even those highly peripheral to the core activities. Suppliers found their commissions drying up overnight. Contractors who had been supplying major customers for years suddenly found themselves out in the cold. They were assured that the abrupt change of heart was nothing to do with the quality of their supplied goods or services; it was simply company policy to manage the vast majority of their operations with the resources they had in-house.

As the recession bit more deeply, however, and companies started to lay off staff in large numbers in downsizing exercises, they found it impossible to manage with the dwindling resources they had in-house. The only way to survive was to seek support again from contractors, outworkers, interim managers, free-lancers and part-timers. In the old days, organizations slimmed down and cut costs by selling off non-core subsidiaries that had very little logical connection with their mainline products or services. Outsourcing, however, offers an alternative route. It involves offloading non-core functions such as information technology (IT) and accounting rather than business operations. Using sub-contractors and outworkers provides an enticing opportunity to avoid the burdensome overheads involved in employing full-time staff. Outsourcing also enables organizations to free up a lot of office space and provides the opportunity to sell off real estate, providing more funds for investment in core activities. This in many ways is a far better solution than the previously popular strategy of downsizing, which had already fallen into disrepute because it had resulted in talented personnel leaving companies in droves, then making companies even more vulnerable to the threatening economic climate. Nor did down-sizing seem to be delivering the promised goods.

Much to their relief, contractors suddenly found themselves in demand again, but neither they nor the companies wishing to use their services quite knew how far the process could go. It had long been accepted practice to contract out such functions as catering and cleaning to specialist firms, but the idea that such critical functions as information technology, or business processes like accounting, administering pensions or answering customer enquiries could be outsourced was a largely new and untried concept.

A report published in June 1998 revealed that contracting-out within Britain's manufacturing industry was on the increase. The report, *Make or Buy?*, based on a survey by The Foundation for Manufacturing and Industry, which covers the whole of Britain's manufacturing industry with a total turnover of £400 billion, disclosed that the outsourcing trend had been extended to research and development, parts of the production process and design. Jane Croot, the report's author, observed: 'Sectors like metal casting, pharmaceuticals and printing, which did not out-source in the earlier periods, have now been doing so.'

The outsourcing trend had already been given considerable impetus by the former Tory government, which used it as a mechanism for reducing the size of the monolithic public sector. Through compulsory competitive tendering, local authorities were obliged to invite bids from external suppliers for functions ranging from street cleaning to collecting council tax.

The majority of National Health Service information tech-nology was outsourced. So were swathes of central government activity, including the Inland Revenue computer systems (where one deal removed 2,000 civil servants from the government payroll). Other outsourced governmental areas included the collection of National Insurance contributions, the Driver and Vehicle Licensing Centre in Swansea and the computer systems that process payments of social security benefits.

It was later suggested by some observers that the Tory government had placed too much responsibility, and perhaps too much power, in the hands of third-party contractors such as EDS (Electronic Data Systems) which picked up some multi-million pound deals. There were questions raised about whether security and confidentiality could be guaranteed when public records were being handled by a company based in the United States. By then, however, the outsourcing bandwagon had started to roll. There have also been some major outsourcing deals in the private sector. Examples include the £50 million contract between British Gas and Cap Gemini to run the utility's main frame computers; the £345 million deal over ten years between Sears and Andersen Consulting to supply the retail group's computing requirements, which later had to be unravelled as a result of a demerger; and a £200 million agreement between Asda and IBM to run the supermarket's IT systems for a seven-year period.

According to the report, *Outsourcing the Finance Function,* published by Accountancy Books, Xerox signed a global ten-year £2 billion contract with EDS involving the transfer of 1,300 staff. BP Exploration is reported to have made savings of 35 per cent as a result of a four-year IT contract with Andersen Consulting which involved taking over 320 staff. Others, however, have been a little more guarded in embracing the benefits of outsourcing as the latest panacea, perhaps recognizing the pitfalls involved.

When the Labour government came to power it was predicted that it would be much more cautious in its outsourcing policies than the Tories, particularly in view of its stated hostility to compulsory competitive tendering and its concern about possible breaches of confidentiality when government information is placed in the hands of private contractors. However, New Labour appears to be as committed to efficiency in government spending as its predecessor and outsourcing can be expected to play a pivotal role in this resolve.

It was reported in a May 1998 issue of *The Times* that around 2,500 jobs at National Savings were targeted as part of one of the largest outsourcing deals ever struck by government – and the largest since Labour came into office. The newspaper reported that the information had emerged from confidential bidding documents obtained by *Computer Weekly,* the trade magazine. Two companies – EDS and Siemens – were reported to be shortlisted for the £1 billion contract. Helen Liddell, economic secretary to the Treasury, was expected to decide on the award later in the year.

It was predicted that more than 4,000 of National Savings' 4,200 staff would transfer to the private sector company. The only parts of the agency not to be privatized would be sales and marketing, although Logica already handles the running of the

Ernie computer, which chooses winning numbers for Premium Bonds.

According to *The Times*, the internal documents showed that EDS considered it could run National Savings with just 1,500 staff, or even less. EDS was attempting to soften the blow by suggesting to National Savings that it could retain and redeploy many of the excess staff within EDS's UK operations.

It was suggested in the *Times* article that the government would try to present the outsourcing solution as preferable to a business process re-engineering plan previously drawn up by the chief executive of National Savings in the autumn of 1997, which estimated that the agency should lose 1,500 staff. The revelation of that plan provoked the Public Services, Tax and Commerce Union into taking strike action.

Unresolved questions

Outsourcing, in both the private and public sector, continues to raise a number of still largely unresolved questions. What other activities are ripe for outsourcing? How do companies define what is core? By historical importance? By the strategic opportunities such activities offer? By the competencies involved? By the ability of core activities to produce more cheaply or to higher standards than an external provider?

There are clearly risks attached to outsourcing when it is allowed to cut more deeply into an organization's critical support functions. Would it be wise to outsource human resources or corporate relations or financial functions, for example? How can issues of security and confidentiality be guaranteed? What are the implications for staffing in terms of loyalty, rewards and overall costs? There can hardly be anything more disruptive to an individual's career than to wake up one morning to find that the big company department that he or she works for has been handed over to a specialized contractor with an entirely different working climate and culture. Some people might relish the opportunity to work for an organization that is devoted entirely to their professional calling. Others might find the culture-shock traumatic.

Despite such misgivings, outsourcing is growing at an accelerating pace globally and in the UK. Precise statistics on the size of the market are difficult to obtain because such a wide range of activities fit under the outsourcing umbrella. However, figures from the research company Input estimate the global market at $41 billion (£25.6 billion) in 1996, rising to $107 billion (£66.9 billion) by 2001.

An earlier Input survey valued the US information technology outsourcing market at $18.9 billion (£11.8 billion) in 1995, rising to $36 billion (£22.5 billion) by 1999.

Contracts for IT outsourcing in the UK reached £1.5 billion in 1996, up 15 per cent on 1995, according to the IT outsourcing firm ITnet. There were 133 contracts signed in the UK in 1996, with 91 agreed by companies outsourcing for the first time. Analysts expect the UK market for all types of outsourcing to be worth £4.8 billion by the year 2000.

A strategic tool

However, the most significant shift in attitudes to outsourcing is the fact that it is no longer seen by most companies as merely a cost-cutting exercise, but as a strategic tool. Writing in a special supplement on outsourcing in the 28 May, 1997 issue of the *Daily Telegraph*, Nuala Moran notes: 'The search for multiple and strategic benefits signals a new stage in the development of the outsourcing market. Rather than merely a way to reduce costs, it is now perceived as a route to improve business performance and competitive strength.'

A survey by Andersen Consulting of 350 executives, to find out what they expect their companies to look like in 2010, threw up some revealing expectations with regard to outsourcing. While cost-cutting was still the prime motivator for outsourcing, six other highly strategic reasons were proffered: to improve overall business performance; to sharpen business focus; for accessing external skills; for improving quality and efficiency of the outsourced process; to achieve competitive advantage; and to create new revenue sources.

Moran observes that there is an important overall aim behind the move to consider outsourcing appropriate for an ever-expanding range of functions – to move away from rigid, self-sufficient organization structures to open entities with the flexibility to respond rapidly to new markets and new technologies – but she is not among those who predict that the ultimate result of the expanding outsourcing market will be the 'virtual corporation' – a fluid entity, operated by a skeletal permanent staff, that buys in skills, processes and other resources in response to market demand. Moran does, however, see outsourcing in the wider perspective of 'a potent tool for restructuring in the face of ever-increasing competition'.

To a large extent, the degree to which such higher-level expectations are met will depend on how well the process is managed at the boundary between organizations and the contractors providing the outsourced service. Clearly, the relationship between the two organizations has to be a close one and one that is meticulously monitored, particularly in the early stages. All kinds of new approaches are being adopted to build in safeguards. Sharon Smith, writing in the *Daily Telegraph* supplement, notes that in the IT outsourcing market, corporations are increasingly signing global deals and opting for supplier alliances instead of choosing a single vendor for all their needs.

'Part of the trend is driven by the increasingly global nature of the market,' writes Smith. 'But another aspect is that, according to a report by Deloitte & Touche, *Leading Trends in Information Services*, a high proportion of users have been disappointed in outsourcing deals and are striving to improve performance on both sides.' This can partly be attributed to a lack of skilled contract management on the part of outsourcers, and suppliers' failure to understand business needs.

More flexible contracts

Discontent is leading to a shift towards shorter, more flexible and partnership-type contracts. Others have signalled their dissatisfaction by more direct means. The RAC, Virgin Direct and NEC have all brought outsourced functions back in-house, although the RAC insists that in its case it took control again of its complex voice and data network because of its increasing importance to its business. Clearly a case of re-identifying what was core and critical to its success.

Most companies, however, that have taken the outsourcing route and found it falling short of expectations prefer to experiment with the management formula rather than the more costly and complicated route of a large-scale retreat. It is evident that seeking the right ingredients of successful outsourcing is still in its infancy and will undergo a considerable amount of trial and error for a long time to come. The strategic issues for each firm will concern what is core and non-core. The operational issues will concern the process of managing the outsourcing and the external contracts.

These are the issues that will be debated in this book. It will look at outsourcing from the point of view of the organizations that take it on board, the contractors who offer their services and the individuals who find themselves caught up in this new quest for strategic dominance and cost-effectiveness. It will explore the nature of outsourcing, why organizations resort to it and how they go about seeking the most appropriate relationships with contractors. Following the process through, the book will outline how organizations and contractors work together and how outsourced contracts are monitored to ensure they meet expectations. Whether the 'virtual organization' is a feasible proposition or simply an imaginative concept that will remain just that will also be examined.

2
What is
Outsourcing?

The term 'outsourcing' is comparatively new, but the idea of contracting out peripheral functions to third-party providers to allow an organization to concentrate on its core activities has been around for a long time. The major oil companies, for example, have long recognized the advantages of taking this route. During some thirty years' service with Shell, George Lefroy, head of senior management resourcing at the multinational's London head office, saw the workforce halve from 200,000 to 100,000. 'Some of that,' he observes, 'has been Shell recognizing that certain activities that we've done traditionally are far better done by contractors or independent agents. At one extreme there was the whole business of service station operations and supply of the product in lorries to the countryside. Typically, if you go back thirty years we owned and managed the service stations with Shell staff, we delivered every last drop of fuel with Shell drivers in Shell tankers to every last village. We quickly saw that there were some of those activities where we didn't have a competitive edge at all, where contractors or independent businessmen could do a far better job. So typically we withdrew from involvement in many of those activities.'

Similarly, Shell concluded that many aspects of prospecting for oil and designing and constructing offshore oil platforms could better be sub-contracted to specialists. In recent years, it has become obvious that such activities are not core to Shell. As Lefroy explains, Shell now focuses on a much narrower band of core activities: 'We are an integrated energy company and we are also the world's largest petro-chemical company. That's where our core business is and we want to position ourselves with investments and operations such that we can run those businesses either directly or perhaps indirectly through joint ventures in certain countries where we need local partners or other international companies as partners. So we have been gradually, in staffing terms, shedding those activities which are not core and coming back to those activities that are core, and the 100,000 people we now have in Shell run a very much larger business than the 200,000 people we had when I joined the company.'

At one level outsourcing is no different from conventional supply management, but the outsourcing decision is a strategic one and is generally taken at a more senior level. A business function that used to be run in-house is handed over to a third-party specialist to manage.

At its most basic level, outsourcing is simply buying in components that a manufacturing company used to make itself. It is a make or buy decision. Does it make sense to produce a particular component or would it be better to buy it from outside? Other issues follow on from that make or buy decision. What is the cost of making? What kind of capital investment does it involve? What kind of investment does it need in terms of space, capital resources and all those kinds of things? What kind of return can be expected? How does that stack up with a decision simply to buy it in?

Transactional

In this sense, outsourcing can be regarded purely as a transaction. There are an infinite number of suppliers out there, all equipped to produce the identical product, in which case you simply shop around on the basis of price. Provided the supplier's price is lower than what it would cost to manufacture it in-house, it makes sense to buy it from outside. Otherwise, all you are doing is cost-handicapping yourself. A hospital carried out an analysis to figure out what its in-house painters were costing it. When all factors were taken into consideration it was reckoned they were costing around £23 an hour. By outsourcing, the hospital could bring in painters from the outside at a cost of around £12 an hour. When that was added to the problems of office space, providing and storing equipment and keeping it safe, outsourcing was an obvious choice.

However, when you come to specify precisely what you expect from an outsourcing transaction, the issue starts to become rather more complicated. Some of the early examples of outsourcing for services like catering and cleaning were viewed as relatively easy to specify. There are basically two approaches. On the one hand you can specify the contract in terms of output. In the case of an outsourced cleaning operation, you can, for example, specify that there should be no more than one piece of litter within an area of ten square metres at any given moment. How the contractor achieves that target is its problem. Alternatively, the airport or hospital management might say that it wants a specific concourse area swept four times a day. In one instance, you are specifying activity to cover a service level. In the other, you are specifying a result. When the service is provided in-house you are more inclined to focus on a result, because you can make judgements on whether or not you are falling below accepted standards. When you go outside for the service, the contractor is likely to prefer it to be regarded as an activity, because that is relatively more easy to price. The contractor knows exactly what needs to be done to meet the terms of the contract.

The kind of outsourcing agreement you enter into will depend on the kind of relationship you have with the contractor. There are two approaches which are almost polar opposites. One approach is entirely transactional. The contractor simply gets paid for what is done. The contractor is expected to sweep the concourse four times a day. The hospital or airport management sets up a monitoring system and if the concourse is only swept three times, the contractor is only paid for that amount of work.

At the other end of the scale, you can have a relationship where the supplier and the purchaser – the airport or the hospital – understand that in the end what they have to do is keep the customers happy. It doesn't really matter whether the concourse is swept once, twice or twenty-two times a day. The real issue is how the customers perceive it. In order to move to that kind of approach you have to build a partnership. The partnership replaces clear specification linked to payment on delivery with some notion of a relationship. That will involve issues concerning trust and openness and a willingness to be flexible about the terms of the contract provided the end result is perceived as satisfactory to the customers.

How you build a relationship of openness and trust becomes quite critical. For the partnership to work, both parties have to bring something to the table. There has to be a level of inter-dependence that is mutually beneficial. If you can both operate entirely separately and still deliver, you don't need a partnership, but if the contractor needs access to information or people inside the company, there is clearly a need for an approach that is close to a partnership. There clearly has to be inter-dependence.

There is a very obvious example of this in recent trends in supply management. Many companies are reducing the total number of their suppliers, but working in closer partnership with those they have selected. Nissan, the car manufacturer, for example, has evolved a plan with its UK suppliers in which it expects the suppliers to reveal not only the specifications they are working to but financial information as well. Initially, the UK suppliers were horrified. Typically, as a supplier you price your products at a level that gives you a margin. The profit you make is up to you. However, in this case the suppliers were confronted with Nissan saying that unless they opened up their books it would not deal with them.

Achieving a partnership with suppliers involves a complicated thought process, but apparently straightforward transactions are not as clear-cut as they may seem at first sight. Some years ago economists began to analyse in depth the true nature of transactions. If you buy something, what does it cost you? The simple classical answer is that it costs you whatever you pay. In reality, of course, that is a gross over-simplification. Prior to the actual purchase, you may – depending on what you are trying to buy – have incurred research costs, trying to find the right suppliers and trying to get a sense of what the price range is. You may want to do some bargaining and the contract negotiations themselves may be protracted. All that costs time and money.

Asymmetry of information

In addition, there is the issue of asymmetry of information. If you go into a shop and buy a hi-fi system, you are pretty much in the hands of the salesman who advises you, unless you happen to be an expert on the subject. When you get home you may find the hi-fi you have been persuaded to buy doesn't have several of the facilities you would like. Worse still, you may find you have bought a lemon. The shop may, on the whole, sell good hi-fis, but this wasn't one of them. As the buyer you are at a disadvantage in terms of asymmetry of information. So transaction costs can be a lot higher than they appear on the surface. If you are buying from the external market and you have no reliable method of judging whether or not you have bought a lemon, you are vulnerable. If, on the other hand, you make it in-house you can be a lot more certain of the quality of the end product. The balance of information in this case is more in your favour. So there are more factors to consider than simply price.

If you decide to go outside, however, and there seems to be good reason to form some kind of partnership with your supplier, there are a lot of different issues to consider. How much relationship do you want? How much openness? How much trust? How much access? What competencies do you have that you are not prepared to display? Japanese car manufacturers have come to Europe and set up in partnership with western companies. The Japanese have offered better quality cars to European companies that understand the market better. There is a partnership of complementary competencies. The western firms have the marketing and sales skills; the Japanese have the production skills.

In the case of a real partnership, you use each other to go on being very good at your own competence. You don't try and invade the other party's territory, although you may find it entirely appropriate to have some frank discussions with your partner on occasion. On the other hand, you may decide to build a more limited partnership. A lot of firms have outsourced their IT function, for example. In theory what they are outsourcing is the worry about the hardware. They don't have to make the investment in hardware and software and someone else picks up the problems of servicing and supporting the IT function. There are benefits too in outsourcing the IT staff, who are often quite small groups with limited career opportunities, but who now have the opportunity to upgrade their professional competence. At the contractor to whom they have been outsourced, there is much more scope for career development and much more awareness too that they actually operate in a market.

Two ends of the spectrum
Outsourcing means different things to different people. Craig Lardner, group manager, supply management, for the BOC Group, the multinational industrial gases company, cites two examples at opposite ends of the spectrum. BOC's Australian gases company decided a few years ago to outsource its legal

services. 'We were doing a sourcing supply management activity not unlike buying anything else we choose to buy around the company,' elaborates Lardner. 'The head of the legal department in Australia is a lawyer and he has two assistants who are also lawyers, all internally employed. At the end of our legal services outsourcing we still have those three people in place, but the way we secure, manage, measure the performance and pay for legal services is now quite different.'

At the other end of the spectrum, BOC in Australia has outsourced all its information management (IM), apart from applications development, to an outside organization, transferring most of the staff involved. 'There was a time,' says Lardner, 'when most organizations would not be prepared to let go of their information technology facilities and practices, let alone its people, for fear of that being a show-stopper for the business. The concern over not having your own IM infrastructure anymore has diminished to the point where one of BOC's businesses has now very successfully outsourced its IM services, despite quite a few people thinking it was a dangerous move. The applications development staff are basically the only people who are still BOC employees.'

The computer services provider has taken on the total responsibility for setting up BOC employees in Australia with all the hardware and software needed to operate their personal computers. The provider also runs the help desk. BOC pays an agreed price per employee for the service.

The service even extends further. The provider runs a disaster recovery site for BOC in Australia which replicates the company's main computer system in the event of a breakdown that could otherwise bring the business to a grinding halt. The disaster recovery site is at a secret location well away from BOC Australia's Sydney head office and is shared with fourteen other companies. By sharing these facilities the costs are greatly reduced compared with what BOC would have to pay if it decided to have its own separate site.

Lardner contrasts the different approach BOC took to outsourcing legal services and its IM operations: 'The outsourcing of legal services was not about ending up with no lawyers in BOC. It was about utilizing a best-in-class law firm to provide exactly what BOC specified it needed better than BOC could provide for itself. The information management example, by contrast, is taking something that we once held very close to our souls, and never imagined we would let go for fear of the damage it might do to the business, and releasing our people to a provider who can do it better than we can, with the exception of the applications development people.'

An ongoing process

Mike Dodsworth, human resources manager at Cap Gemini UK, one of Europe's leading IT services providers, defines out-sourcing as taking over responsibility for an ongoing process. If a major chemical company approaches Cap Gemini and asks it to develop a sales order processing system, it is tempting to think of it in terms of outsourcing, because the company could have chosen to write the programme in-house, but Dodsworth doesn't see it that way. 'We wouldn't see that as outsourcing because effectively it is a short-term project. It has an end and a deliverable, and that deliverable is the working project. Outsourcing to us would start when a client hands over an ongoing responsibility for something, whatever that might be. It doesn't have to involve a transfer of people, but more often than not it does.'

Dodsworth cites the example of a leading telecommunications group that approached Cap Gemini to help it design a billing system. The client company also realized that it needed a data centre to process all the bills and it did not feel it had sufficient in-house expertise to handle that. It bought all the necessary equipment and set up the system on one of Cap Gemini's data centres and let the experts run it. 'It did not involve any transfer of staff because it was a new service and we employed the people who were necessary to keep the service running. So I would say outsourcing is the responsibility for delivering an ongoing service to defined criteria,' adds Dodsworth.

Specialization, alliances and innovation

According to Graham Winch, professor of business analysis at the University of Plymouth Business School and Stephen Sturges, a partner at Derriford Systems, writing in a January 1998 issue of the *Western Morning News*, outsourcing is 'a reflection of profound and far-reaching changes taking place in organizations across the country and around the world'.

They believe the three words that capture the essence of what is required by organizations as they hurtle towards the millennium to be specialization, alliances and innovation. 'They are at the centre of the transformation from the vertically integrated organization of the past to the networked organization of the future,' suggest the authors. 'Excellence and experience are now recognized as the keys to competitiveness and they are rooted in specialization. Organizational specialization takes many forms; one of the most important is a keen understanding of, and aggressive investment in, an organization's core competencies. Corporations realise that to gain competitive advantage in today's business world, they must transform themselves into streamlined entities concentrated on the things they do best.'

Alliances of all kinds, according to Winch and Sturges, have become the principal means for both nurturing a focus on core competencies within an organization and linking specialities across organizations. Innovation, they suggest, is the final and possibly most crucial dimension. 'Just outsourcing what is already in place does not create lasting competitive advantage. The players involved in these alliances continually exploit the unique qualities of their partnership to innovate new solutions for the ultimate customer. Innovation is the convergence of special-ization and alliances – all taking place under the framework of an outsourcing agreement.'

CO-SOURCING

Malcolm Brown points out in an article in *Management Today* that as well as embracing more sensitive central functions like customer care, outsourcing is evolving in another way. Corporations are thinking about outsourcing complete processes, rather than just discrete functions or activities. Several banks, including the Co-operative, Brown observes, are outsourcing cheque clearance, for example. It makes sense for banks to outsource this particular process since the volume of cheques written is actually in steady decline, making it hard to justify spending time and money keeping the required technology up-to-date. For service providers like Unisys, on the other hand, technology like image processing systems can be used across a range of businesses and a range of customers, so it does not matter that the cheque processing business of the individual bank is declining.

The move towards process, writes Brown, could be important for another reason, namely that it is easier to measure the inputs and the outputs of a particular process than of individual functions or activities, such as information technology. It is easier to define what is going into a process and what you expect to come out. The fact that most major companies are now re-engineering themselves around processes rather than functions would also suggest that the drift towards process outsourcing will continue.

It is not just what is being outsourced that is slowly changing, however, but also the way in which that outsourcing is conducted, notes Brown. Some pioneers are trying out variations such as *co-sourcing*. For while traditional outsourcing may be perfectly suitable for low-risk peripheral activities such as cleaning or car fleet management, with higher risk strategic functions or processes, companies want to retain more say in the way in which the work is done. With co-sourcing, the client company keeps responsibility for the management and strategic aspects of the outsourced activity, while the outside provider supplies consultancy services and, often, experienced personnel to help the business streamline the function or process.

Karen Hamilton-Smith, a partner in international executive services at chartered accountants Arthur Andersen, cites expatriate administration as one of the areas that lends itself to co-sourcing. 'The company may wish to retain involvement in the selection process and in deciding the detailed terms and conditions of an overseas assignment, within the context of management priorities. But outsourcing the handling of all aspects of the administration of the assignment – such as determining allowances, preparing cost projections, conducting orientation classes, co-ordinating relocation, payroll and accounting matters and providing ongoing support to the expatriate and to the management – is a sensible strategic alternative.'

The financial group Société General (SG) has an outsourcing (others might call it an insourcing) arrangement with Arthur Andersen, under which an Andersen tax expert spends two days a week in the group's human resources office to advise senior management and expatriates on taxation issues. Louise Barrett, SG's head of human resources, distinguishes co-sourcing from classical outsourcing. 'In outsourcing another organization takes responsibility for the particular function – in this case managing expats – and therefore all the liaison is with the external organization. *Co-sourcing* is where responsibility is held within the organization, so the person from Andersen is actually here in my department, part of my team and interfacing with the procedures and practices of the department.'

(The above information, together with references in subsequent chapters, is extracted from an original article in the January 1997 issue of *Management Today* with the permission of the copyright owner, Haymarket Publications Ltd.)

STRATEGIC SOURCING

John Little, an outsourcing expert at PA Management Consulting, believes it is possible, by studying the most successful outsourcers and seeing what they have in common, to isolate certain characteristics which might improve a company's chances of having a successful outsourcing policy.

The best companies, Little says, take a strategic top-down approach to outsourcing – he terms it *strategic sourcing* – and are clear and disciplined in their decision-making and process management. Most outsourcing is done in a fairly piecemeal fashion, often for tactical reasons. Strategic sourcers, by contrast, outsource because they can see benefits for the wider organization. 'Organizations which are more sophisticated take a strategic decision to enhance their core competencies, which might well look the same, in terms of gaining access to skills and so on, but is done with quite a different strategic intent,' says Little.

PA researchers think that companies like Nike and Virgin (particularly in the latter's approach to the new world of finance in the shape of PEPs) are good strategic sourcers.

STRATEGIC INSOURCING

An American remedy for the often fraught relationship between managers and human resources professionals was highlighted in an article written by Margaret Coles in the 20 April, 1997 issue of the *Sunday Times*. The method, known as strategic insourcing, involves putting training into the hands of a specialist company that sets up camp on the client's premises (not unlike the travel services *implant* referred to in Chapter 5).

The concept was developed in the US by DuPont at its headquarters in Wilmington, Delaware, and is being made available in the UK by the Forum Corporation, based in Boston, Massachusetts. Edward Trolley, a Forum vice-president, is DuPont's former head of training. He says: 'We had a training and development organization of about 100, and were also outsourcing to thousands of companies. But our senior business leaders said they were not delivering business value. They said we measured our success by our levels of activity rather than our business impact.

'They said training focused on programmes that taught skills, but they needed it to relate to business issues. We recognized that training and development was critical to success, but not one of our core skills. We decided we must find a partner that was world class at training and development and bring it inside DuPont to live with us, merging it with the best people on our staff.'

Forum was chosen, and in the first year the list of thousands of courses – including fifty-four for time management – was cut severely. Trolley says: 'We created the role of relationship manager, a business person who knows about training, employed by Forum but working inside DuPont. He identifies business issues and puts together options for the client, who decides whether to make an investment.'

Three years after setting up the DuPont programme, Trolley joined Forum to market the concept he had helped to devise. 'Because we're inside the organization, we're living with our clients, walking the halls with them, attending their planning sessions, understanding their business inside and out. Once we know what they're trying to accomplish, we can determine whether people need new skills, deliver the appropriate training and then measure whether the business result was achieved,' says Trolley.

'We sign a contract which records the business result the client expects to get: it may be two percentage points on revenue or a one per cent increase in market share. The client is billed for the services he uses and if he is not happy we'll redo what we've done or refund the money.'

The Sharewatch column of the 13 July, 1997 issue of the *Sunday Times*, edited by John Waples, referred to another example of what might be construed as strategic insourcing. It pointed out that the Prudential planned to hand over management control of its investment technology to Andersen Consulting, in a major shake-up of the insurance company led by Sir Peter Davis. Under the move, almost 1,200 Prudential employees were scheduled to switch over to a new company, which would be owned by the Pru but headed by an Andersen Consulting partner.

SHARED SERVICE CENTRES

Internal outsourcing might sound like a contradiction of terms, but in fact a number of companies are setting up shared service centres (SSCs), which could be described in this way. Although such centres remain within the corporation, they have a high degree of independence that allows them to act in a manner similar to an external outsource provider.

'A shared service centre is an independent organizational entity which provides well-defined services for more than one unit (which may be a division or business unit) within an organization,' explains Peter Moller, a London-based business consultant with Arthur Andersen, responsible for co-ordinating shared services work across Europe. 'The SSC is responsible for managing its costs and the quality and timeliness of the services it provides to its internal customers. It has its own dedicated resources and typically will have informal or formal contractual arrangements, often called service level agreements with its customers.'

In an article for a report entitled *A Business Guide to EMU*, sponsored by Arthur Andersen in association with Treasury Management International, Moller offers the following definition of an SSC: 'People are often confused as to the difference between shared services, outsourcing and centralized financial functions. Outsourcing is a term used to describe locating financial activities in a legal entity outside of the corporation itself – i.e. another company will provide your financial services.

'Although the move to a shared service structure may geographically look very similar to a move towards centralization, the two concepts differ in a few important ways. Whilst centralized finance functions tended to be heavily oriented to, and controlled by, corporate headquarters, shared services are typically outward oriented towards their internal customers. The customer focused culture with an SSC is usually reinforced with service level agreements that ensure service standards and cost levels are continuously monitored and improved.

'The service level agreement is used as a vehicle to charge out the SSC's costs to its customers – ensuring the SSC is fully accountable to them. Best practice SSCs use activity-based costing to price the products and services provided accurately and allow customers to manage the costs charged to them better, for example by changing from a paper based supplier invoice process to EDI (Electronic Data Interchange).

'In a centralized finance function you rarely find the same customer/supplier relationship and business units will typically feel they have little say in the cost or quality of the services they receive. Indeed, some SSCs will give their internal customers the choice of going elsewhere for their finance and administration services, and the SSC itself may look for customers outside the organization (i.e. become an outsourcer to other companies).'

Ciba Speciality Chemicals took the SSC route in 1996. In March that year Dr Michael Jacobi, CEO designate of the new $6 billion Swiss multinational company, which had been formed as a spin-off after the merger between Ciba Geigy and Sandoz, was faced with the task of designing a completely new finance function. On the one hand he had the opportunity to start with a clean sheet of paper and design a world-class finance function, but on the other hand he needed to ensure Ciba Speciality

Chemicals had a fully operational finance function in place by 1 January, 1997. The solution that he felt offered the greatest efficiency and effectiveness was SSC. 'We simply could not afford to go on processing invoices in the sixty-eight sites around the world that existed at the time of the spin-off,' says Dr Jacobi. 'In addition to the high cost, service levels provided by each of these sites to their business were variable and, as no two general ledgers were identical, the reporting information produced was difficult to compare and consolidate. We decided on a global shared services solution as the only way to significantly reduce overall costs, standardize data and maintain, if not improve, service levels.'

PARTNERSHIPS

Premises and facilities management is probably one of the most widely outsourced functions. According to The Centre for Facilities Management at the University of Strathclyde, it can account for 13 per cent of total purchasing costs in commercial organizations and it, too, is undergoing some fundamental changes in the way that it is outsourced.

The trend, according to Geoff Tyler, writing in the 2 October, 1997 issue of *Supply Management* magazine, is firmly toward all-in contracts, especially with the advent of intelligent buildings. If the contractor puts in replacement parts at its own expense, it will look after the plant more carefully. The Benefits Agency, for example, has used Symonds Facilities Management under contract to manage work on the structure, fabric and installed services of 157 of its buildings. The work includes planned and responsive maintenance with SFM providing mechanical and electrical engineering, interior designs, building surveyors, architects, quantity surveyors, *et al*.

The unusual feature of the Benefits Agency's relationship with SFM has been the management of the buildings and their installed facilities in a partnership. Management is done by teams consisting jointly of BA and SFM executives, located on BA premises. Projects are prepared for competitive tendering quickly with the benefit of on-board experts to help evaluate the tenders received. The partnership teams also use remote monitoring of building management systems and a 24-hour help desk to provide a fast reaction to developments.

The Benefits Agency, via BA Estates, went out to tender in 1997 for a total business management outsourcing contract which was won by a consortium led by Goldman Sachs and including the Symonds Group.

Another company that has taken the partnership route is Benetton, the Italian textiles giant. When it was formed in 1965 it had to adapt the traditional small-scale structure of Italy's textiles industry to an organization capable of competing in world markets. Design skills were the company's strength, but the founders had only limited resources so they created an operation based on partnership that came close to being a virtual organization: manufacturing was handled by small workshops throughout northern Italy while selling was licensed to entrepreneurs who bought the goods.

This strategy for tackling the global market has helped to build Benetton into a business selling through more than 7,000 shops in 120 countries with a turnover of more than £1 billion by the early 1990s.

3
Core and Chore

Ask most managers what functions they believe are most suitable for outsourcing and the inevitable answer will be non-core activities. Ask them to elaborate on the difference between core and non-core and they are often stumped for an answer. They simply haven't thought it through.

Observes Bob Aylott, head of KPMG's outsourcing advisory service: 'Core is a label that people attach without sufficient thought. Most businesses don't understand what is core. What is core today may not be core in ten years' time. The core and chore argument, in my opinion, is over-worked. It is a neat phrase that has some appeal, but under scrutiny it is quite difficult to justify. It tends to be what people think they can package up with some degree of definition.'

Information technology, Aylott suggests, is one such function that can be neatly packaged in this way. Added to that, it is the cause of a lot of frustration that managers are only too happy to pass to an external expert to sort out. IT can be expensive, take too much time to master and people don't understand it. Far better to put it in the hands of someone who can make a better job of it.

This is a view echoed by Ron Coomber, sales administration director at Carlton TV, which outsourced its air time booking system from the outset: 'Carlton had no intention of setting up its own large in-house IT department – it sees itself as a media company, not an IT specialist. Only the sales staff themselves are Carlton employees. Everything else – through bookings, slot allocation and charging – is done by an IT facility outsourced to Cap Gemini.'

The application software was an existing Cap Gemini package, heavily adapted for the project. In addition to those changes, Carlton specified a service quality level of 98.5 per cent system availability which, Coomber says, they have capped by achieving 99 per cent.

Denis O'Sullivan, an IBM consultant, sums up his view of core and chore in the following way: 'I suppose one of the things you should look at is whether it is critical and whether it is being done as well as it can be. If it is critical and you are not doing it as well as you can, you either have to do it a lot better or find someone who can do it better for you. It really needs to be looked at from the point of view: how important is it? If it's not important, then that may be a good argument for outsourcing it because you don't want to waste management time and effort on it. If it is important and you can't do it well, find someone who is an expert and can do it better for you.'

Mike Dodsworth, human resources manager of Cap Gemini UK, observes that for some companies IT is core while for others it is not. 'Certainly the banks in general would regard IT as a core part of their business,' he suggests, 'because you can hardly operate a bank these days without IT skills. If, however, you're a brick-maker or a major pharmaceutical company, is IT really part of your core business? You need it to keep the business going, but you also perhaps need a staff canteen and a security department – and those are the sort of functions that are getting outsourced. The only people who are being retained these days are those who fall into the category of business analysts, who lay down the strategy of where a company needs to go. Once the strategy is defined, they hand over the tactical and then the operational delivery to an outsourcing company to continue.'

Aylott argues, however, that outsourcing should not merely be a matter of handing over to experts those functions which you would rather not do yourself or which cause too much hassle. To think in those terms when outsourcing IT is dangerous, in his view. 'IT is critical to all the business processes that operate within an enterprise. Take finance, for example. You cannot think about finance these days without the underlying IT. They're indistinguishable. IT is part of the finance function. So from a strategic point of view, you should ask whether you ought to be into business process outsourcing.'

The core and chore argument is a popular concept, easily grasped, but, as in the case of a lot of simple ideas, the reality is somewhat more complex. In some respects, the initial analysis when deciding what can or ought to be outsourced shouldn't be difficult. Can this operation be done more cheaply in-house than the market can provide it for us? Is there a cost advantage from doing it in-house? If there is, there seems little point in outsourcing it. If a particular part of the operation can be carried out more cheaply in-house than if it was bought from the market, while maintaining the same level of quality, there is a potential competitive advantage.

Thinking about the make or buy decision when considering core and non-core, it makes perfect sense to favour the idea of buying non-core. Does it make sense to make non-core? It could. For a variety of reasons you might be better at it than outside suppliers. If you are, it could be an area of *unexploited competitive advantage*.

If you have identified something as core, does it make sense to buy it? You may not actually have any choice if you are unable to perform the function really well. There's a difference between what's core and what's *critical*. One definition of core might be the functions you perform for yourself when you have some real competitive advantage in the market. There are other things that may be critical, but in which you have no market advantage.

Human resources might be considered critical, but you may be dissatisfied with the way your HR department is functioning. The HR department may be failing to recruit the best people for you. Production design might be critical. The way it actually looks, how customers react to it, might be critical, but you may not be happy with the skills of your product designer and consider going to an outside design house. So there is a difference between what is core and what is critical. There may be areas that are critical in terms of your ability to deliver a product or service to the market place, but in which you have no core competence.

Deciding what is core to your business will always give rise to considerable debate. Views and interpretations will often differ. It might have been thought, for example, that a good public restaurant plays a core part in attracting customers to a major retail store and that it should therefore be managed internally. However, Littlewoods announced in the summer of 1988 that it would be contracting out the running of its ninety in-store restaurants to Granada, the media and catering group, in a deal that would see 2,000 staff change employers. The seven-year agreement with Granada Food Services was said to be worth £375 million in turnover and was believed to be the UK's largest multi-site catering contract. Littlewoods had clearly decided that Granada had the greater expertise and that by outsourcing the operation it could concentrate on its core retailing activities.

Continuous improvement

The BOC Group does not believe in deciding which functions to outsource by simply looking at its core competencies. Outsourcing decisions emerge from a broader continuous improvement mentality. BOC scans all its business areas to examine how they might be performed more efficiently and cost-effectively. In the supply management function it found that there were 253 areas of expenditure amounting to a global spend of £2.6 billion, ranging from travel to information technology and legal services. It explored each of these 'buckets of spend' looking for continuous improvement opportunities.

'When you first look at it, your problem is not finding the opportunities; it's getting all the opportunities in order of priority,' says BOC's Craig Lardner. 'By taking this approach we ended up with an immediate twenty-five projects out of the range of 253 opportunities.'

The twenty-five selected priority projects were then further scrutinized to try to decide which of them would make the most impact on the organization and which were the most practical proposition in terms of reaping real benefits. That process whittled the shortlist down to about ten projects and within those ten opportunities BOC identified a number of areas where outsourcing could be expected to achieve the kind of improvements in quality of service and cost-effectiveness the company was seeking. 'We didn't start out by asking which areas we should outsource. We started out examining the full scope of continuous improvement opportunities, ending up with a number of those that offered outsourcing opportunities,' explains Lardner.

Like many organizations, BOC had recognized that certain corporate activities are obvious candidates for outsourcing. A predictable example is staff catering, but the continuous improvement exercise has thrown up areas of outsourcing that BOC probably would not have considered before. Says Lardner: 'At the end of the day the organization's test as to whether it is in a better state than it used to be is primarily two measures – the total cost of what it now incurs versus what it used to incur, and the overall quality of service it is getting compared to what it thought it was buying.

'I don't have much enthusiasm for the idea that what is or is not a good outsourcing opportunity should just be based on core competencies. If you want to take it to the nth degree, the core competency BOC starts with is separating molecules. It takes a cocktail called 'air' and it separates it into all its different constituents. You could say that is where BOC's core competency is at its most polished because freighting, moving the gas, you could argue, is not a core competency. It is of TNT and all those freighting companies, but as it happens BOC has built up a competency in distribution of the gas that helps it add value to the supply chain better than an outside transport company can. In that case, our core competencies have been extended to include distribution of gas.

'You might then say that is where our core competency must finish. That is not true either, because the use of gas, its application in the market, could in fact be a core competency of a gas company if it chooses it to be – and we do. So you now have three links in a domino effect – making the gas, distributing it and applying the gas – and BOC has a core competency right across that line because it chooses to.'

Central functions
According to research by The PA Consulting Group, the average number of functions outsourced by organizations has risen 225 per cent (from 1.2 to 3.9) over the past five years and will go on growing. At present the most frequently outsourced activities are property services, catering and information technology, but there's now clear evidence that outsourcing is moving from peripheral activities towards more central ones.

Historically, for instance, it was thought fine to outsource payroll, a relatively repetitive and simple operation, but not such sophisticated functions as treasury management. Now, however, according to the Economist Intelligence Unit, as many as 10 per cent of companies may be outsourcing treasury. Similarly, while property services have been outsourced since sub-contracting began, now, according to PA, more than 10 per cent of organizations are outsourcing property management as well, and some are even farming out their property portfolio.

All the indications are that this particular trend may go a lot further, maintains Malcolm Brown in an article on outsourcing published by *Management Today*. 'Classical outsourcing theory says that a company should decide which of its functions give it competitive advantage (its core competencies in management-speak) and which don't. Non-core functions can be farmed out to specialists if they conduct them more cheaply or better or both, but core functions never. To outsource core functions, say the theorists, is to hand over the things which make the company what it is – and which make its profits.'

Increasingly, however, this rule is being questioned, observes Brown. It is now argued that there has been a confusion between core activities (things that are central to what one does) and core competencies (the central things that one does well). Those who take this line now talk about outsourcing functions like customer care, an activity which most outsourcing theorists would consider so central to a company's success that only a lunatic would hand it over to a third party. If you cannot look after your customers, say the traditionalists, should you be in business at all? Aren't customers the *raison d'être* of every business?

Mark Astbury, sales and marketing director of Ventura, a company which handles customer service management for companies like Kingfisher, Cellnet and the Co-operative Bank, understands people's surprise that organizations should be prepared to entrust such sensitive work to outsiders, but the practice is not so odd as it first seems, he says. 'Cellnet, for instance, have said to themselves, "What are our core competencies?" and they've come down firmly and said their competency is running a mobile phone network, that there are other things they don't regard as a core competency and one of those is customer service. Customer service is a core activity, but they've decided to find a partner who can help them manage customers better than their competitors do and, crucially, better than they believe they can do themselves.'

At the level of things like customer care, says Astbury, there's a difference between outsourcing because you cannot do something yourself and outsourcing because you want to be the best in the market place and you need an expert to help you. 'People, I think, now understand that you're not simply outsourcing because you can't do it, you're outsourcing because there's a partner who can help you to be the best in the market.'

Mike Webb, managing director of Mondial Assistance, which provides claims hotlines for a number of insurance companies, also argues for a redefinition of the concept of core business. If you take an insurance company, he says, the instinctive thing to say is that a company which can't administer its own hotline can't be relied on to carry out its business effectively. 'But that's obviously nonsense. The company's responsibility is to assess the risk that each customer represents and provide them with the most appropriate and cost-effective package of cover. It is also the company's responsibility to ensure that its spread of risk leaves it in a position to pay out claims where necessary. Investing in these skills is a cost-effective use of resources, but staffing the claims hotline is not.'

The risks inherent in outsourcing customer care are not that different from those involved in factoring, a form of third-party debt-collection that existed long before outsourcing ever appeared on the scene. Companies that hesitated to use a factoring service to collect outstanding debts feared that their relationships with important clients might be jeopardized by the heavy-handed tactics of the third-party agency. However, factoring as a concept has grown steadily over the years as companies have discovered that handing over the time-consuming chore of chasing money to a third-party agency, experienced in debt-collection techniques, has helped to improve their liquidity, and in some cases has saved them from bankruptcy. In addition, the factor acts as a middleman, saving the company from any embarrassing personal contacts with slow paying clients. As with outsourcing in general, factoring enables companies to concentrate on their core activities.

Ring fence?

This inevitably raises the question of whether there is an irreducible core of activities which could not or should not ever be sub-contracted. Is there a ring fence around certain activities or functions such that anything inside is sacrosanct and untouchable? The experts differ on this, notes Brown in his *Management Today* article, and will do so even more as once-inviolate activities like treasury management and customer care are increasingly outsourced. One attractive rule of thumb is to consider what it is that managers would absolutely have to keep in-house if they were starting the company from scratch, and outsource everything else. Another way is to identify which parts of the company constitute the corporate crown jewels. A pharmaceutical company, say, might well consider outsourcing research and development on drug delivery systems and the controlled release of drugs in the body, but would never dream of farming out research into the selection of the molecules involved in the drugs.

Even then, there are dangers. The definition of crown jewels may change over time, says Dr Chris Lloyd, who runs consultant Arthur D. Little's technology and innovation management practice in the UK. 'In computers,' he says, 'the crown jewel element was the hardware, so IBM outsourced the software, the operating system, to the little known Microsoft because they thought the operating system was a minor, peripheral technology. Then over time, they found it was the operating system which became the crown jewels and what they were left with, the hardware, was the peripheral technology.'

Getting to the core

There are three main ways that organizations can approach outsourcing, depending on how cautious they want to be:

Firstly, there is what might be called *the onion-peel approach*. This is the method adopted by organizations that want to test the waters before they commit wholeheartedly to the concept. These organizations steadily peel off the more peripheral functions, such as catering, cleaning and car fleet management to outside agencies, confident in the knowledge that if, in their inexperience they make mistakes – by picking the wrong contractors, for example – no great damage will be caused to their core activities. This is a prudent approach that understandably has been taken by a lot of organizations that are biding their time to see how successful outsourcing in general has been in delivering its promised benefits. The disadvantage of this cautious approach, of course, is that it will not initially make a significant impact on an organization's cost-saving goals and it will not necessarily prove the case for outsourcing one way or the other.

Even if this initial toe-in-the water approach proves successful, it does not automatically mean, when it comes to peeling the next layer and penetrating more deeply into the onion, that the organization concerned will be free of risks. The lessons learned in peeling off the outer layers might be helpful, but as the organization works its way towards the core of the onion the risks will inevitably be higher and it will still be in unknown territory. However, this layer-by-layer approach does have the advantage that an organization can more easily reverse an outsourcing decision when it discovers it has gone about things in the wrong way. However, in terms of an immediate impact on the bottom line or a new corporate strategy, this is not a fast-track solution.

A more immediate effect can perhaps be achieved with what might be termed *the bite-out-of-the-apple approach*. This is where an organization decides to be more adventurous and outsource a critical function, but one that is not necessarily core to its operations. It might reason, for example, that its IT operations, though vital to the efficiency of the organization, can best be handled by an external provider whose specialist knowledge could never be replicated in the organization itself. There is undoubtedly a fairly high level of risk attached to handing over such a critical function to an outside agency – if the contractor gets it wrong it can virtually bring the outsourcer's operations to a grinding halt – but by researching the market carefully and selecting the right contractor, the outsourcer can relieve itself of a substantial overhead and place it in the hands of a provider whose specialist knowledge is a distinct advantage.

The test for the outsourcer is making judgements about how much risk is being taken and what the impact could be if the contractor does not come up to scratch. For example, many organizations might hesitate before handing over their customer care department to an outside agency for fear that it could result in the disruption of carefully-nurtured client relationships. Organizations should also think twice about outsourcing what is undoubtedly a non-core activity, but one which represents an unexploited competitive advantage. A company's transport fleet, for example, may well be regarded as non-core, but over the years it may have built up such a high degree of logistics expertise that it can offer this to third parties and profit from it. It would be foolish, in an attempt to cut costs and streamline the organization, to outsource an activity where the profitable gains could far outweigh the internal overheads. That would be throwing the baby out with the bath water.

Organizations that are anxious to see quick results from taking the outsourcing route may have little choice but to take large chunks out of the apple, while keeping the core – but they need to be sure they are the right chunks.

The really brave organizations are those that are wholly committed to outsourcing and take the third way, *the striptease approach*. These organizations, once they are convinced that outsourcing works, regard it as a strategic tool (not simply cost-cutting) and adopt it as their credo. They waste little time in stripping away all non-core activities and arriving at what is a stark, uncluttered organization focused on its main function in life – producing goods or a service (although the production process might itself be outsourced). Organizations that take this uncompromising route may well have chosen outsourcing as an alternative to another strategic tool that has failed to deliver the goods. They may, for example, have attempted to streamline by introducing business process re-engineering techniques, but switched horses when BPR seemed to be causing undue trauma without delivering the desired changes. The discovery of outsourcing may have come as the answer to a prayer when other techniques seemed to be letting them down. Already committed to wholesale change, they may have decided that there was little to be gained in going about outsourcing half-heartedly. It is all or nothing.

The risks are obvious. At the end of the striptease, such organizations may find themselves embarrassingly exposed when they discover they have lost control of key functions to outside providers that fail to demonstrate the degree of innovation and creativity that was expected of them. In their haste to embrace the outsourcing credo, these organizations may have been less than thorough in their market research and picked the wrong providers. Or they may not have set out clearly enough in the contracts with these providers precisely what they expected to gain from the transaction. They could find themselves fighting too many battles on too many fronts.

On the other hand, if they get it right, these stripped-for-action organizations, unencumbered by the heavy armour of non-core clothing, can expect to enjoy a sense of operational freedom that allows them to tackle the market place utterly unfettered. It goes without saying that this approach requires a considerable amount of courage and entrepreneurial flair, as well as an ability to pick the right agencies. It is perhaps not surprising that Richard Branson is considered by many to be one of the masters of this kind of approach.

At the extreme end of the spectrum, such organizations perform a disappearing trick and become virtual. Run by a remote handful of central office staff, they are little more than a brand name. They are the last vestige of the incredible shrinking company.

4
Why Outsource?

Initially, outsourcing was regarded almost exclusively as a useful way to cut costs. Manufacturers such as toy firms and the makers of electronic goods have long recognized the competitive edge they can secure by outsourcing large parts of their production processes to cheap labour in developing countries. Nike, the sports goods giant, for example, does not itself make any of those world-famous trainer shoes. They are produced by 500,000 assembly workers in thirty-one different countries around the world, a large proportion in South-East Asia. Some of these outsourcing manufacturers have been highly criticized for exploiting poverty conditions in countries less well off than their own. Nike, for example, came under close scrutiny in a BBC Radio 4 environmental programme, which suggested that the wages it paid factory workers in places like Indonesia were pitiful compared with its $900 million a year marketing budget. A spokesman from Nike in the UK responded that his company had always followed a policy of paying the mandated minimum wage in whichever country it employed labour and that the marketing budget was spent on creating a demand for its products, which in turn helped to improve the living standards of its worldwide army of assembly workers.

Whatever the morals of the issue, the cost-savings resulting from handing over labour-intensive manual tasks to sweat shops in countries on the other side of the world has long offered economic advantages that few mass-production manufacturers have been able to ignore.

Advances in technology have helped to increase dramatically the amount of outsourcing that is carried out by service industries. Modern telecommunication techniques have paved the way for teleworking, which allows people to perform mundane administrative tasks from remote locations and at cheaper cost than if they were performed at the centre of operations with high overheads. For example, American insurance companies have found that they can cut their over-heads significantly by farming out the processing of claim forms to teams of administrative workers in Ireland. Modern tele-communication techniques mean that the processing can be undertaken by these teleworkers on the basis of a 24-hour turnaround.

The popularity of outsourcing has grown even more rapidly as it has become apparent that other cost-cutting devices, such as business process re-engineering, are failing to deliver the desired benefits. Hiving off non-core activities to an outside organization, which can often involve all or the majority of a function's workforce, is seen by many organizations as a near painless way to reduce overheads at a stroke. It has the additional advantage of freeing up management to concentrate on those areas of the organization where it has the most internal expertise. Increasingly, however, outsourcing is being seen as a strategic tool with much wider aims than simply cost-cutting.

Make or buy?

A report produced by Jane Croot for The Foundation for Manufacturing and Industry has identified some interesting trends in the way outsourcing is evolving in the UK. Based on a comprehensive survey of ninety-five industrial sectors in the UK with a total turnover of £400 billion, the report, *Make or Buy?* reveals that during the early 1980s to early 1990s those industrial sectors that were the most profitable experienced the highest growth in outsourcing. This finding, Croot observes, is the opposite to conventional wisdom that decrees that the least profitable companies are the most likely to resort to outsourcing.

'This result puts a new light on profitability as a driver to outsourcing,' concludes Croot. 'It suggests that during the 1980s outsourcing was a strategic decision to maintain profitability and competitiveness, rather than used as an *ad hoc* method to reduce costs and make short-term financial improvements in those less well-performing industries, as has been suggested in much of the literature.'

However, Croot's findings indicate that in more recent years the less profitable sectors of the manufacturing industry have woken up to the benefits of outsourcing and it is these that are now experiencing the greatest rise in its application.

Croot's research has also revealed that international exposure is a significant characteristic of outsourcing companies. 'Those sectors that have a higher level of international exposure have seen a higher growth in outsourcing, suggesting that international competition is a driver to outsourcing. This might be the case for a number of reasons. Firstly, those sectors more exposed to international (and thus more) competition may need to put more effort into ensuring and maintaining a competitive position and, assuming that it cuts costs and improves competitiveness, outsourcing is a way to achieve this.

'Secondly, the more internationally exposed sectors may have access to a greater number of competitive suppliers from both at home and abroad, making outsourcing a more profitable decision. Finally, those sectors with little international exposure tend to be more insulated from the latest best practice and management techniques, which consistently in this period advocated outsourcing.'

Croot also found that the industrial sectors with relatively larger levels of administrative workers experienced a much larger rise in outsourcing during the 1980s. This, she argues, was to be expected for two main reasons: 'Firstly, during the 1980s it was the labour intensive activities, and particularly those undertaken by administrative workers, that were outsourced, such as catering, cleaning and later IT, rather than manufacturing activities undertaken by operative workers, which are more capital intensive.'

Secondly, there was much rationalization of labour during this period, not only throughout the business in general to improve productivity, but also in downsizing where whole management levels and functions were got rid of. 'In many cases, firms experienced difficulties with the restructuring and large layoffs this involves and outsourcing was seen as one solution to get rid of the problem and "pass the buck" to someone else.'

Croot's deduction is that it is probable that firms outsourced in the 1980s to reduce labour costs and commitments, rather than to reduce capital investment requirements and fixed costs, as much literature and evidence has suggested. However, in the latter period of the study those industrial sectors with a higher ratio of operatives to administrative workers have been experiencing the greatest growth in outsourcing. 'The direction of outsourcing may be changing in this period with firms either having already outsourced labour intensive activities or choosing to outsource those that are more capital intensive, such as parts of the manufacturing process. As this change in the type of outsourced activity occurs, so too do the drivers of outsourcing. In the 1990s outsourcing may be driven more by strategies to reduce capital and investment risks, obtain specialist input and reduce fixed costs than was the case in the 1980s.'

The general conclusion that Croot draws from her study is that the reasons why UK manufacturing firms have been adopting outsourcing as a management tool have evolved over the 1980s and 1990s. 'Between 1982 and 1995 outsourcing in manufacturing has not been a purely random process,' she observes. 'There are characteristics particular to those manufacturing sectors that have experienced the highest growth in outsourcing. However, these characteristics are not all consistent over time, but change, often gradually, in a particular direction, throughout the time period. A change in the type of outsourced activities from services to more capital intensive activities may be influencing some of the labour characteristics, whilst previous growth in outsourcing may be another influencing factor on characteristic changes.

'High profitability and international exposure are characteristics of those companies that had the highest growth in outsourcing during the 1980s. Rather than outsourcing being used as a quick-fix or a solution for under-performing companies and sectors during the 1980s, it has been a strategic decision by the most highly competitive and internationally-exposed manufacturing sectors (such as motor vehicles, office machinery and computer equipment).

'However, as the general level of outsourcing has risen throughout the 1990s, the analysis suggests that outsourcing is increasingly a strategy adopted by less profitable sectors (such as the manufacture of fabricated metal products and machinery). It is possible that a positive experience of outsourcing in the more profitable sectors in the 1980s and the spread of best practice is leading to a more widespread adoption in the 1990s.'

The evidence gathered by Croot suggests that outsourcing, which was once a strategy adopted by highly profitable, internationally-exposed and labour intensive manufacturing sectors, is now a strategy undertaken by manufacturing sectors which cannot be so easily classified. 'In the 1990s outsourcing growth has been greatest in those sectors with a low initial level of outsourcing (such as manufacture of aircraft, printing and pharmaceuticals), many of whom did not experience the rise in outsourcing of the 1980s. These sectors are neither particularly profitable nor labour intensive and it is possible that by the 1990s outsourcing has become a more widespread strategy not identifiable with any particular sectors or outsourced activities.'

A key force

A survey of 350 senior executives around the world, published in 1987, concluded that outsourcing will become a key force in shaping enterprise in the twenty-first century as more companies recognize the need to strip out internal functions which prevent them from concentrating on their core markets. Commenting on the survey, conducted by the Economist Intelligence Unit in association with management consultants Andersen Consulting, Nuala Morgan observes in a *Daily Telegraph* supplement on outsourcing: 'While at present managers rely on mergers and acquisitions as the chief tool for restructuring companies, in future they will look to federations of joint ventures, collaborations and outsourcing to achieve change.' She adds: 'This represents the maturing of outsourcing, an activity originally conceived blatantly as a way to reduce overheads on functions such as catering, cleaning, refuse collection and managing the company car fleet by farming them out to specialists.'

Bob Aylott, head of KPMG's outsourcing advisory service, argues that outsourcing decisions should be part of an overall corporate strategy rather than considered as isolated cost-cutting exercises. 'Our ideal model is when somebody comes to us for a sourcing strategy – should I improve the efficiency internally or should I look to the market to help me achieve all or part of my aims? The outsourcing strategy internally may be that you decide to go for shared services or break them up and put them back into the business units, for example. But out of that would normally come a clear decision with some rational objectives and base-line target costs. That would be our preference because normally we would want their objectives to be much wider than simply cost reductions, although we would normally expect that to be one of the objectives.'

That ideal model is rarely the starting point for organizations seeking an outsourcing solution, however. All too often, managers have not really thought through their reasons for outsourcing or what they would like the end result to be. In Aylott's experience, managers' outsourcing objectives are normally rather simplistic single goals such as cost-saving, but increasingly, he finds that the decision to outsource is based on a desire to bypass internal politics. 'Almost every situation I've seen so far is really shared services that could have been done internally, but it would never have got through internally because of internal politics. Take it outside the organization where it has only commercial pressures and it gets done. I can think of one client who outsourced all its financial activities across Europe, and really all that was needed was two, or maybe three, shared service centres.'

The client wanted a system of standardization across all the businesses with economies of scale. By ripping it out of the organization and handing it over to external experts all the hassle of internal wrangling over who would be responsible for what and what policies would be adopted were dealt with at a single stroke. 'That wasn't written down as an objective,' points out Aylott, 'but in practice it was the rationale behind the decision. Most outsourcing of finance has been done on this basis.

'The real motive is cost reduction or systems replacement or systems standardization for corporate information purposes, or things of that kind, but the reason for choosing outsourcing as against shared service centres internally is politics. One ought to expect the external supplier to be better than the internal service as well. So it should enhance the cost-saving over and above that which could be achieved were it to be done internally.'

The true motivation, in Aylott's experience, is preserving

business empires at a time of corporate restructuring. For instance: 'I want the service to run out of Brussels and therefore my people won't get fired – all your people do. It will operate on my site and therefore I will get a contribution towards my overheads as against out of London where I give them a contribution towards their overheads.'

Aylott says: 'With outsourcing you wipe it out of the discussion. But in practice the objectives we try to get people to think about are much wider than that – access to innovation, skills and experience of other organizations, best global practice. So you need to choose a supplier who has those capabilities – best systems practice, previous experience of implementing chosen software. All those things at the end of the day lead in part to lower costs, but to other things as well.'

In many cases organizations choose to take the outsourcing route because they recognise that contractors like Cap Gemini have a far higher level of expertise than they could ever achieve – or perhaps want to. Mike Dodsworth, of Cap Gemini UK, cites the example of an insurance group that felt its own IT staff were not able to keep pace with an ambitious programme of new systems development. The insurance company therefore arranged to transfer its staff to Cap Gemini which it knew had the expertise at its fingertips. 'One of the things we would say about outsourcing is that it turns what is a fixed cost for an in-house environment into a variable cost, because in any in-house environment there will be peaks and troughs in the workload,' points out Dodsworth. 'But unfortunately you have to pay for the people whatever the level of the workload. One of the messages we put across is that our clients pay only for what they want.'

When providing an IT applications management service, Cap Gemini agrees a contract with the client company that recognizes that a core group of, say, ten people will always be needed to keep the service running, but that the two parties will sit down at regular intervals to decide if additional resources will be required in the months ahead to meet an upsurge in demand. In the case of the insurance company, there is a core team of the people transferred to Cap Gemini that can be topped up from Cap Gemini resources whenever the occasion requires it.

GLOBAL COMPETITION

In the view of Professor Graham Winch, increasing global competition has forced many businesses to focus their energies on activities vital to creating and delivering core products or services. In the article he co-wrote with Stephen Sturges for the *Western Morning News*, he suggests that for many companies 'the further an activity is from the delivery of its products or services, the more managers have to question and justify its cost effectiveness.

'The more distant an employee's job responsibilities are from producing or delivering the organization's products, the more probable it is those activities could be performed more cost-effectively by an external provider. The increasing costs of benefits, higher skills, payroll taxes and salaries are forcing companies to look for alternatives to direct employment. In today's world, no one person can keep up with all the changes involved in managing the organization's most costly and important resource – its staff. Combine this with the pressure on businesses to be both lean and profitable, and you can see the "squeeze" this puts on the manager who is accountable for profitability. As a solution, many executives have turned to outsourcing.'

The trend towards globalization is encouraging many international companies to reduce their number of suppliers in a wide range of services, and in some cases to a single global supplier. This in turn is leading to outsourcing to suppliers with whom strong relationships have been developed. An example of this evolution can be found at The BOC Group, which is steadily outsourcing an increasing number of non-core activities such as travel and legal services, as part of a fundamental reappraisal of its supply management policies and practices. The drive behind BOC's move to outsourcing is undoubtedly cost-effectiveness, but it also aims to improve the quality of the service by placing it in the hands of a dwindling number of experts who have come through the company's strict analytical and selection procedures.

BOC's annual purchasing spend is £2.6 billion. A one per cent improvement in the way the company buys in goods and services equates to a four per cent improvement in profits. By 1997 some thirty-one projects had either been completed or were under negotiation with suppliers, amounting in total to potential benefits of £25.5 million. These projects related to purchases totalling £595 million, equivalent to 23 per cent of BOC's spend in 1995/96.

One of the goals of supply management is a fundamental switch away from the old-style purchasing function involving head-on negotiations with a large number of suppliers in an attempt to beat down the price. With supply management the trend is to reduce the number of suppliers drastically and, where possible, to form mutually beneficial partnerships with world-class suppliers.

The suppliers most likely to win BOC business are those that can offer consistent global or regional service. In some cases, the reduction in the number is dramatic. In the UK, for example, the number of temporary employment agencies BOC deals with has dropped from 102 to just two. Says Tony Isaac, BOC's group financial director: 'That is probably an extreme case. Cost improvement is a major objective, but other objectives are to achieve a better service, quality and cash flow. In order to do that we need to get a much more meaningful relationship with a smaller number of credible suppliers.'

One-stop shop
The trend towards globalization is giving rise to the emergence of 'one-stop shop' outsource providers that can offer a consistent,

high quality service all over the world. One such global service provider is MSX International, the US-based $1 billion turnover company that can boast 11,000 employees and contract personnel in twenty-three countries. 'Through its single source, full-service approach, MSX International provides its customers with a key advantage over the competition. We provide a global service and can support customer operations anywhere in the world,' claims Don Springer, the company's vice-president, business and technology services.

MSX International's historic market was the automotive sector with clients that included many of the world's major car manufacturers. The company has since branched out into other sectors, including insurance, healthcare and defence. It now provides a one-stop shop outsourcing service for key business processes, including:

• automated procurement systems, order status and expenditure tracking, supplier performance measurement, supply base management and reporting capabilities
• comprehensive marketing support programmes, including customer satisfaction surveys, data management, premiums and incentives, customer loyalty programmes and warehousing and fulfilment
• electronic document management, offering conversion of documents and drawings into an electronic form, archiving them and making them available through Internet or intranet services; customer publication help desks, web publishing and hosting
• turnkey, tailor-made managed training programmes
• warranty process management and administration, dealer process improvement and dealer management programmes, plus business administration programmes
• flexible staffing solutions, from single employee sourcing to managed staffing programmes, providing staff and managing supplier networks

• engineering programmes from virtual prototyping to full vehicle models, manufacturing consultancy, technology product development services

MSX International claims to add value to its customers' businesses by identifying, implementing and managing cost-effective processes, enabling companies to achieve their strategic business objectives. Its innovative solutions for enhancing a client's administrative systems through process improvement programmes have a measurable positive impact on the business while helping to build customer loyalty, it maintains.

'We are constantly applying technologies and innovative processes in our areas of expertise to help our customers easily access critical information, reduce costs and reduce cycle times in their business. These process improvements also help build customer loyalty. Outsourcing enables customers to concentrate on their core activities,' says Springer.

Global training

Comprehensive training programmes that can be applied across any industry is another service provided by MSX International that appeals to globally-oriented organizations. The company has developed tailored training programmes for customers like Procter & Gamble and Caterpillar and its multimedia delivery methods allow both large and small-scale training programmes to be implemented cost-effectively.

The company's global managed training services range from needs analysis to implementation. With a database of 3,500 training experts, its services have a broad application to a wide variety of skill centres. Many levels of service, from outsourcing of an entire training programme for a company to technical training for plant operation for supervisors, can be tailor-made to meet the client's needs.

MSX International suggests that the benefits gained from joining it in an outsourcing partnership include 'elimination of competing demands on a company's business, enabling it to concentrate on its critical core business activities. It can also provide a stimulus to increasing creativity. Practical improvements noticed by our customers include more efficient handling of logistics and administrative detail and greater integration of human resource department functions.'

LOGISTICS

Logistics was probably one of the first areas that looked ripe for outsourcing. As Carol Debell points out in a *Daily Telegraph* supplement on outsourcing, companies that realized in the 1980s that they were saddled with expensive vehicle fleets and warehouses were enthusiastic about divesting themselves of these assets. Distribution firms were seen as the opportunity to transfer some of the fixed costs into variable costs.

A decade later, observes Debell, it looks as if some of the flair and innovation has gone out of the industry. A survey by the Institute of Logistics, whose members include hands-on practitioners and academics, found dissatisfaction among many of 300 companies that had taken the outsourcing route.

Denis O'Sullivan, an external business transformation consultant with IBM, who helped to compile the survey, says that many of the 300 companies polled made it clear they wanted more from the relationship than they were getting. 'They are looking to providers to offer a much more strategic and innovative input in the development of their distribution operations,' he says.

The trend towards outsourcing logistics is nevertheless expected to continue. O'Sullivan's experience points to an overriding reason for this. 'It is quite clear from dealing with major clients around the world that the supply chain is one of three key areas which they see as vital for the development of the business of the future. The other two are customer intimacy and the management of the knowledge that allows you to run that efficient supply chain – they all fit into the same area.'

O'Sullivan describes logistics as 'the management of the physical movement of goods and the management of the information and the relationships which are necessary to help them work together. Another way of expressing it is that the physical movement of wheels and the provision of depots is not the driving force behind logistics. That's an output. The driving force should be the relationships between the partners in the supply chain. In a retail supply chain, for example, you have the manufacturers, the retailer, the consumer and you may have a wholesaler. It's combining all that, so that you can achieve greater efficiency by working together than you could achieve if each sector was working in isolation. If it is an internal supply chain, it means working together across the functions rather than in each individual functional area.'

Companies have been using third-party transport companies long before the term outsourcing was coined. Some fifteen years ago, as more and more companies realized that transportation was not a core part of their business, two different approaches emerged. One was to sell off the transport business and many of the biggest transport operators today in third-party logistics came from hived off in-house operations. The other approach was to outsource the transport operations that were not big enough in their own right to form a separate company.

It came as a relief to many companies to shed these assets and hand them over to a third party, because, in O'Sullivan's view, transport and warehousing had always been an under-managed part of many organizations. 'It was an area where many companies really had no great interest. A lot of the managers tended to be operators who had come out of the business themselves. The transport manager may well have been a truck driver or a warehouse manager may well have been a truck driver. They weren't given the necessary training to take them forward and develop the operation to the next stage of sophistication.'

Breaking down barriers

There is nothing new about outsourcing when it comes to moving products around the world. Debell points out in her *Daily Telegraph* article that the issue was never about ownership of planes or ships, but about managing the shipping process, which traditionally has been done in-house. Now these barriers are breaking down.

It is the supply chain that has made the difference. For years logisticians have theorized about taking control of the chain. That theory is at last being put into practice, notes Debell. Companies are looking for seamless service that controls products from the factory shelf to the final destination.

Many of these chains are complex, involving the movement of raw materials and components to manufacturing and assembly points, then finished goods to destinations all over the world. The third-party providers which have grasped this opportunity are the large forwarders. Already highly experienced at providing the core activity – the transport leg – these companies are now ensuring they can provide the additional services that turn traditional freight movement into a complex logistics package.

The distribution arm of The BOC Group – BOC Distribution Services (BOCDS) – is a good example of this evolving process. BOCDS has been distributing food products to Marks & Spencer stores throughout the UK for more than a quarter of a century. BOC's pre-eminence in the production of industrial gases and the development of food-chilling technologies made it ideal for the purpose. The industrial gases company's core activities fitted it well to take charge of a function that allowed Marks & Spencer to concentrate on what it does best – retailing.

More recently, BOCDS has expanded services first developed exclusively for M&S to develop new customer outlets, while at the same time broadening its activities for M&S. In 1997, BOCDS was awarded a contract to manage the complete warehousing and distribution requirements of the M&S franchise in Korea. A new BOCDS subsidiary, BOC Distribution Korea

Ltd, was formed to handle this addition to the long-standing partnership between the two groups.

Other recent developments have seen BOCDS branch out into extensions of its conventional services and the launch of some completely new businesses. Some of them have taken it into new regions of the world far from its traditional home-based logistics business in the UK. The new ventures have included the setting up of an independent air cargo handling operation at Melbourne Airport, the initial phase of a Aus£20 million business development in Australia. That has coincided with the launch of a new freight management service which involves working in partnership with customers, enabling BOCDS to gain a more in-depth understanding of the supply chain.

The partnership with M&S began in 1969 when BOCDS acquired the family firm of G.L. Baker, which had been distributing food products on behalf of M&S for thirty-seven years. Over the next twenty-five years M&S's business naturally diversified and its distribution needs became more complex. The era of chilled foods made BOC an ideal partner in meeting M&S's distribution needs.

The transportation of M&S's chilled food employed the Polarstream system of refrigeration, which used liquid nitrogen as the cooling agent. This avoided using a diesel engine and its associated emissions. The system had the distinct advantage of being silent, which meant the food could be delivered to M&S stores in residential areas at all hours with the minimum disturbance to the people living and sleeping there. An added bonus was that the Polarstream technology uses no CFCs and HCFs and is therefore environmentally friendly.

The development of the Polarstream technology was also a great boon to BOC. Until then liquid nitrogen had been regarded pretty much as a waste product for which there was very little practical use. Suddenly there was a chance to sell large quantities of a product that previously had very low value.

Peter Brinsden, managing director of BOCDS, observes that

the birth of the partnership with M&S was a happy coincidence of desires: 'A number of things came together. There was obviously a developing rapport; there was liquid nitrogen and Polarstream technology; there was the M&S desire to increase its food business significantly. In 1969 its food turnover was £86 million a year. It is now £2.4 billion. M&S had clearly taken the view that building a serviceable food business, focusing particularly on chilled foods, needed the right infrastructure.'

BOC Transhield was formed in 1970 specifically to handle and expand M&S's chilled and ambient food distribution. It now handles 90 per cent of M&S's fresh, chilled and ambient food products from six strategically-located regional centres, delivering it to some 300 M&S stores throughout the UK. It is believed to be the largest operation of its kind in Britain.

The concept of delivering fresh foods in the quickest and most economical way, using intermediary depots, was pioneered by BOCDS and M&S and has since been copied by many other transportation companies. BOCDS and M&S were also the first to develop the concept of product consolidation and secondary distribution with a fully integrated handling system for foods – trays, handling pallets and vehicles, all designed to reduce handling time.

By using intermediary regional depots, it has proved possible to co-ordinate deliveries much more effectively and to avoid the traditional congestion caused by countless supplier vehicles converging on stores in crowded town centres. It has also given M&S more storage space at its stores, enabling it to extend display areas.

The success of the Transhield operation led in 1985 to the formation of Storeshield, a dedicated BOCDS service for delivering textile goods to M&S stores in Scotland and the south of England. BOCDS now distributes some 20 per cent of M&S's general merchandise.

The partnership has kept pace with the latest developments in information technology in order to maintain a high level service.

There have had to be sophisticated levels of communication all the way along the supply chain. For example, bar code readings at the check-out counters in M&S stores now automatically provide stock and sales information on which to base distribution decisions. This attention to perfecting the links in the supply chain has given M&S a vital competitive edge.

At a celebration at the London Transport Museum in September 1994 to mark the twenty-fifth anniversary of the partnership, Sir Richard Greenbury, chairman of M&S, said it would be hard to find a better illustration of a successful partnership than the achievements of the previous twenty-five years between the two companies. He added that nobody could have foreseen the full extent of the growth of the M&S chilled food business. 'For this we needed to have complete confidence in the food chain, from the raw materials supplied right through to the till point. The temporary storage of chilled foods and their transport on to the stores had to be in the hands of excellence.'

Like a marriage

Richard Giordano, who was then chairman of BOC, commented: 'At the risk of over-working an analogy, ours has been like a marriage. We have on occasion been furious with each other, sometimes not even talking, but for the most part we have worked together to make the best of what we have, often expressing support and occasionally admiration of each other. In fact, I would guess the logistical links that bind us may even be a bit more durable than some contemporary marriage vows.'

The long-lasting partnership between BOC and M&S is clearly one that illustrates how outsourcing can work well and to both parties' advantage. But O'Sullivan stresses that any company considering outsourcing its logistics operation should be clear about the reason for doing so. The first thing he asks a company that seeks his advice on how to go about it is why they are intending to do it in the first place. In the past it was often simply because it was the fashionable thing to do. This is rarely the motivating force today, but companies still tend to consider outsourcing logistics because it is a problem that they want to offload on to somebody else. If abdication is the prime motivation, O'Sullivan warns the company that they will be asking for trouble.

'I tell them that it is wrong to outsource a problem. What they should be outsourcing is an efficient operation. It is wrong to say they are not prepared to take the trouble to make their operation more efficient, that they will simply outsource it. If you do that you won't end up with an efficient organization. The fact that someone can save you ten per cent doesn't mean the operation is efficient, it just means it is cheaper. The third-party service provider will achieve the savings somewhere but it won't mean they are running the business any better. If you have a major problem in terms of customer service, for example, and the third-party company continues to run your logistics operation the same way that you did, the problem is not going to go away. It is just going to become more difficult to control and keep a handle on it.'

IT OUTSOURCING

BP Exploration, the British Petroleum Company subsidiary, is held up by many as a model of an enlightened way to go about outsourcing IT operations. Its IT operations have since been integrated with those of BP's other main business streams, but the outsourcing exercise it went through in the mid-nineties still provides some fascinating insights and important lessons. The aim was to cut costs, gain more flexible and higher-quality IT resources and focus the IT department on activities that directly improved the overall business. BP Exploration had concluded that it no longer needed to own the technologies that provide business information to employees. 'The market for technology services had matured during the previous decade and it now offered companies like ours a broad array of high-quality choices,' observes John Cross, who was head of IT at BP Exploration at the time and now performs that function for the whole of the BP Group, which in August 1998 announced its Amoco merger plans. 'Additionally, the problems encountered in most internal IT departments, with their mix of old and new machines and skills, and their traditional tendency to focus on technological details rather than on business issues, distracted our management and frustrated executives. We believed the market place offered us an opportunity to trade ownership for results.'

BP Exploration did not, however, consider outsourcing to be an end in itself, but part of a broader initiative to re-shape its IT department. In 1990, the company's IT department supported a staff of 1,400 people. Through outsourcing and consolidation that was reduced to around 100. Those that remained were increasingly engaged in activities 'that create real value for the organization, such as working directly with business managers to suggest technologies that will improve business processes, cut costs or create business opportunities', as Cross puts it.

'We want the IT department to help improve business, not be an internal group whose mission is to respond and supply,' Cross wrote in an article in the May/June 1995 issue of *Harvard Business Review*.*

BP Exploration did not take the fashionable route of handing over all its IT operations to a single supplier, because it believed such an approach would make it vulnerable to escalating fees and inflexible services. On the other hand, Cross was anxious not to divide the company's IT operations into discrete slices and outsource all or some of the pieces. It had previously experimented with selective outsourcing and discovered that the disparate contracts required far more management resources than they were worth.

*extracts reprinted by permission of *Harvard Business Review* from 'IT Outsourcing: British Petroleum's Competitive Approach' by John Gross, May/June 1995 issue. Copyright © 1995 by the President and Fellows of Harvard College; all rights reserved.

Beginning in 1989, BP Exploration had contracted selected IT services from a few small and a few large providers. Several of the contracts had delivered the benefits the company had hoped for – reduced fixed costs, improved service and access to new ideas and technologies. 'But the big picture was another matter,' recalls Cross. 'Our contract with suppliers did not provide them with incentives to co-operate with one another. As a result, suppliers managed their own little slices of the pie quite well, but the task of managing inter-contract problems fell to us.' The company found itself constantly adjudicating technical issues or solving problems that fell between the cracks.

BP Exploration has since been integrated with the Group's other two major business streams (Oil and Refining) to form one global services unit under Cross's leadership. At the end of 1997, BP as a whole went back to the drawing board and embarked on a review of lessons learned from past experience in an attempt to redefine its expectations from the outsourcing market.

PROCUREMENT

One blue-chip company in two is considering outsourcing all or part of its procurement, according to a MORI poll for Price Waterhouse (now known as PricewaterhouseCoopers). The survey of over eighty European and US companies with a turnover exceeding $1 billion (£595 million) found that more than half have considered outsourcing the buying of indirect materials such as office supplies, and that almost 60 per cent of European businesses have considered outsourcing their total purchasing function.

Cutting operational costs was the main driver, with 12 per cent reporting they had already outsourced some or all of their purchasing. Commenting on the survey, Denis Kenny, at the time head of European procurement outsourcing for Price Waterhouse, told *Supply Management* magazine: 'In five years' time, procurement will be as ripe for outsourcing as advertising and distribution.'

Respondents to the survey – which covered senior-level purchasing directors from manufacturing to retailing – said that the expected benefits of outsourcing the function were better quality of goods and services (17 per cent), more efficient/quicker processing (17 per cent) and better internal customer service (12 per cent). The three most likely barriers were organizational resistance, issues surrounding change management and cost. On a personal level, the main concern about outsourcing was loss of control – which was mentioned three times more often than job security, the next biggest worry.

Added Kenny: 'The message from our key clients is that they are more interested in outsourcing the procurement of low-complexity goods and services which they can buy off the shelf. With higher complexity items that are bespoke and specific to the client, there is not as much advantage. These are the big ticket items that go into the final product or give competitive advantage.'

Peter Parry, a partner at Sterling Management Consultants, told *Supply Management* that he was surprised that half the respondents were considering outsourcing: 'There's an important distinction to make. You could say that by placing all your business for one particular type of purchase with one supplier you are outsourcing it. This is very different from outsourcing the purchasing function itself. In a trading environment, where companies stand and fall by their ability to buy competitively, it is very difficult to delineate purchasing because it is a core function.'

However, Brian Court, a director and senior consultant with PMMS Consultants, in the Viewpoint column of *Supply Management*, challenges the whole idea that procurement can be outsourced. Describing it as 'another purchasing fad looming on the horizon', he takes issue with the idea that a saving in operating costs is a major driver for outsourcing procurement. 'If we assume that costs are two per cent of total spend (at the high end) and reduce them to half, then the cost reduction is equivalent to one per cent of the spend,' he argues. 'But bigger opportunities arise by reducing cost on the spend itself. There are many examples where undisputed savings of 20 per cent to 30 per cent have been realized on specific projects. Overall savings of around ten per cent are achievable on the purchasing portfolio. This is ten times the saving in operating costs.'

Court goes on to argue that benefits of this magnitude can only be achieved by developing innovative approaches to the supply market and close collaboration between all parties. 'But is this possible if a third-party supplier is responsible for purchasing? Will the engineers and other specifiers be more inclined to involve purchasers early on when the potential benefits are highest? We have enough barriers between functional groups in the same organization. Why will this be overcome by outsourcing?'

Court also questions the claim that outsourcing results in better quality procurement: 'Those involved in strategic purchasing know that real improvements in quality follow enhanced buyer/supplier co-operation and mutual understanding. All parties in both organizations (engineers, production, finance and purchasing) need to be closely involved. Will this be enhanced by the addition of a third party?'

Court concedes that there may be some truth in the claim that outsourcing can result in more efficient, quicker processing, but he adds: 'Even this assumes that the host is poorly organized and that the contractor is super-efficient and knowledgeable. This may present a real opportunity for all the low-value, low-risk items in the portfolio, but these typically amount to no more than two per cent of the spend.'

The claim that outsourcing leads to better internal customer service is again disputed by Court: 'Does this mean that the contracting company will comply with all the wishes of internal customers? What if the internal customer seeks action which is not in the overall interest of the business?

'All commercial organizations need an effective purchasing process. Effectiveness is maximized when many functions participate in this development. For low-value, low-risk items, it is possible to contract out to an organization with excellent systems and low labour costs. However, extending this to key goods and services may deny a company the competitive edge it seeks.'

BANKING

Mention outsourcing to most British banks and they will likely cite the office-cleaning contract at headquarters. In an article for the *Daily Telegraph* supplement on outsourcing, Mark Meredith cites the Royal Bank of Scotland as probably the only one in Europe which has seen the profound changes that come from deciding to let someone else handle functions that are basic, but no longer strategic, to success.

Meredith quotes cheque-clearing as an example: 'The Royal has hired a Texan company, EDS, to process its cheques. Radical? For Britain, yes. But EDS already processes more than two billion cheques a year for over 1,000 banks worldwide. It operates in forty countries, and is about to tie up a similar big handling contract in South Africa.'

In the sweeping changes in banking today, points out Meredith, processing cheques is gradually being left behind in terms of core activities. Increasingly, transactions are carried out electronically, through direct debit or credit cards or through telephone-banking and electronic-banking systems. Cheque transactions are dwindling and so is their significance to the bank's business.

Getting another organization to handle them is still a brave move, as Harry Richardson, an executive director of EDS, concedes: 'It's an emotional decision. When you've been processing cheques for 180 years, it's hard to let go. For many banks there are whole areas of management where there are vested interests in maintaining empires. Yet they have been going through tremendous change. There are new delivery mechanisms, such as telephone banking, and new networks, so a lot of processes which used to be core activities for a bank no longer are.

'A bank needs strong leadership – a chief executive who understands the need for change. Banks have been through a cut, slash and burn process attacking costs, and taken out all they could. Now they have to come to terms with the more fundamental and emotional decisions about what core banking is and what it has become.'

Bob Baldock, a partner at Andersen Consulting, agrees: 'British banks and building societies must outsource some of their transactions processing if they are to become lean enough to cope with the increasingly dynamic market place we are in. They have no choice – they face enormous competition in this sector, not only from each other but also from new entrants such as the supermarkets. Recently, six American banks realized that between them they had enough cheque-processing capacity to serve the whole of the US. So together they have created one specialist cheque-clearing organization, with which each has established contracts.

'Banks can't survive simply by duplicating what each other does. Instead, they should be concentrating on the activities that will differentiate them in the minds of their customers and give them a competitive edge. Every night shift workers turn up at banks to process thousands of cheques accumulated that day. It is time-consuming work and often the technology is out of date.'

Meredith notes that EDS, in its contract with the Royal Bank of Scotland, will develop new methods and electronic applications to speed up cheque-clearing. Since many of the cheques handled by a bank are those of rivals, the use of third-party companies processing cheques for several banks at a time makes good sense. Cheque clearing is just the beginning for British banks. Companies such as EDS are also involved in electronic clearing for credit cards, which they see as the next big outsourcing field.

PAYROLL PROCESSING

Plymouth University contracted out its payroll processing in 1997 to the private sector in a deal worth more than £200,000 over three years. The university, one of the largest in the country, with almost 3,000 staff, has outsourced the function to the European IT services group, CMG. The deal signals the end of a local authority arrangement with Devon County Council to process the university's payroll.

The university took the outsourcing route with the aim of producing greater control over its payroll function and improving access to management information. A spokesman for CMG, which has won a number of other contracts in the further and higher education sector, told the *Western Morning News* when the deal was announced that it represented 'a major market success for the firm'.

Plymouth University has four campus sites and employs nearly 2,200 permanent and term-time monthly-paid staff, up to 500 contract-based claims staff and over 250 weekly-paid personnel, split between full and part-time. Payrolls are being processed on a main frame system at CMG's data centre in Feltham, but there are also plans to install a networked system at the Plymouth campus. This will allow local input and access to payroll data and could provide the basis for integration with other computerized applications.

There are long-term plans to link the system to the university's personnel and accounting departments. The new system will allow the university's payroll staff to respond more quickly to management queries without resorting to time-consuming paper systems.

PREMISES AND FACILITIES MANAGEMENT OUTSOURCING

It is a widely-held view that premises management is a function every company should outsource. 'Why on earth are companies whose expertise is the manufacture of electronic chiplets, sexy motor cars or insurance policies, devoting a measurable portion of their energies to trying to run the building which happens to house their activities?' asks Geoff Tyler in an article in the 2 October, 1997 issue of *Supply Management* magazine.

'Some thirty years ago,' he adds, 'I worked for Associated Electrical Industries (now part of GEC), and then Schweppes in a premises management position. Even then, the in-house unit had continuously to call in outside help. We were more co-ordinators of others' expertise than managers. Buildings these days are much more specialist affairs. Offices are becoming semi-intelligent with cabling structures alone which have more capability than TV studios or defence command-and-control centres of only ten years ago. Factories and warehouses are increasingly being designed and built expressly to house the plant and machinery used within them.'

Managing the problem of keeping such places in good condition is no longer a general purpose function, suggests Tyler. Far from being passive people containers, premises today are regarded as having an active role in an organization's quest for ever greater efficiency. Outsourcing the lot means the management contractor alone is responsible for any drop in quality, while an inexpert in-house manager will forever be trying to adjudicate between individual service suppliers' protestations of innocence.

Tyler proffers a counter-argument, however: losing direct control of a vital management function, the failure of which could mean the organization has nowhere to continue its activities.

He quotes in his article Ken Smith, director of Workplace Management, who is at the sharp end of the premises management outsourcing work for, among others, ICL. 'The biggest block on premises management outsourcing is more emotional than fact. There is the job threat which the existing facilities manager sees, of course, but more than that is the trust involved in giving away direct control over a support area critical to the organization's success.'

Tyler concedes that the trend towards the outsourcing of premises and facilities management does have its sceptics. He cites research by contractors Mitie Group Plc which found 85 per cent of companies with over 200 employees want to keep facilities management in-house, though they would contract out packages of the facilities services themselves. Eight per cent intended to keep everything in-house and another eight per cent did, or intended to, contract out the total facilities management function. However, in that last category, few considered premises management to extend far beyond the traditional, physical services areas.

5

The Mechanics of Outsourcing

The first thing a company planning to outsource one of its functions needs to do is decide exactly what it hopes to gain from the transaction. If it is not clear in its own mind about the performance standards it is seeking and the benefits it hopes to gain, how can it expect the provider to do a satisfactory job? When BOC Gases in Australia decided to outsource its legal services, its first move was to survey its internal users to find out what their expectations were. 'It's not what the purchasing managers want, it is what the users want that matters,' declares Craig Lardner of BOC. 'You can't be too clear about the service performance standards you want to buy from the supplier. The more clear the specification is, the less non-value added activity you get later, the less arguing, the less ambiguity. You will avoid all the disputes about who was going to do the innovating, for example. The specification needs to be up front and, above all else, you need to put measures in place so that both parties can see that it is fulfilled. There is no good including innovation in the specification without agreeing at the outset how you are going to measure it. In a year's time when you complain that the supplier hasn't been innovative enough, the supplier is going to say there is plenty of evidence of innovation, but it may not be the type of innovation you had in mind.'

The attributes BOC requires from its outsource provider are built into a model known as SESPA, which it uses to select the supplier and to monitor future performance. SESPA stands for supplier evaluation, selection and performance appraisal. 'SES is picking the winner. PA is measuring the winner's performance over the years against the same attributes with which they won the business,' explains Lardner. If, for example, one of the required attributes is innovation, the supplier is asked to include in its proposal what it believes it can offer in that regard. BOC as the customer then assesses the provider's submission for appropriateness, practicality and value. The supplier is scored on that attribute with an importance weighting applied (which is also determined from the internal users). The supplier who goes on to win the business is subsequently measured against what it said it would provide in the way of innovation and each of the other pre-defined attributes.

Perhaps inevitably, BOC has found its suppliers are often surprised to find themselves subjected to such a prescribed process. The first reaction tends to be dismay at the vast amount of work required in proving their case, but this is soon tempered with the realization that it is in their best interests to clarify their suitability or otherwise for the outsourcing. 'They express two things,' says Lardner. 'Firstly, concern at how much work they're going to have to do to be so specific in response to SESPA, but, secondly, they are very impressed with the rigour that it provides for the process that they're then involved in, which is trying to win some business. One of the things they always say at the end of the exercise is that it was so revealing to them to look internally at themselves through our SESPA model that they can see perhaps some weaknesses they never knew they had. They also discover some strengths that they were unaware of, but which turn out to be quite competitively differentiating for them, something they never appreciated before.'

The exhaustive scrutiny that prospective suppliers have to undergo is never regretted by those who win the business, claims Lardner. 'Not just because they've won the business, but because they take out some other value from having gone through the rigour – i.e. understanding their strengths and weaknesses from a completely different perspective called a customer.'

BOC's approach to its suppliers is diametrically opposite to the traditional approach to purchasing of keeping everything under the table and negotiating for the best price in the dark. BOC lets the bidders for its business know from the outset the attributes it is seeking. 'We include the attributes we are going to measure the suppliers on in the request for information (RFI),' points out Lardner. 'The traditional way would be for a purchasing manager to hide those for fear of the supplier actually getting it right! The traditional purchasing guy would keep that deep in his drawer until the supplier submitted its proposal. Then the traditional purchaser would try to do a comparison against what the supplier had to guess the customer wanted versus what the supplier knows he wants to buy. Our view is to tell the supplier all that up front, because if you want them to put their best foot forward, they must know exactly what it is you've decided you want to buy. It's not an insignificant task to define exactly what it is you are buying, but rewarding because the supplier is then in a position to say whether or not it can deliver. Just saying you want to buy a legal service is totally inadequate.'

Lardner also takes the view that the best outsourcing deals have no expiry date. 'My ideal and default position on these is that they are indeed evergreen. Both parties can have an out clause – and I don't mean thirty days out. It should be around six months, but the intention at the outset for both parties must be that this is now going to go on for ever and that if the supplier making the bid doesn't win it now, it never will, because the winner will get to keep the contract, and they are going to keep it because we will work with them on their faults and they will work with us on our faults. We are not going to ring them up and shout at them down the telephone because they are not up to the mark. We are going to talk to them about why they are scoring low and what we as the customer can do to help them as the supplier to do a better job.'

The SESPA process is continually evolving with added refinements. Suppliers are regularly hitting the mark in terms of providing the very precise performance standards to which they have committed. 'If that wasn't the case, SESPA wouldn't be working,' says Lardner. 'If we had a situation where suppliers were not finding themselves able to meet what it was they said they would do, then there would be a flaw in the SESPA model as to how we picked them in the first place.

'The second comforting piece of evidence for me is that we have not yet once had to sack a supplier we've picked through SESPA. That's a pretty crude measure and even if we had to unstitch one contract because we had got it wrong I wouldn't unstitch SESPA. We would investigate what it was we must have done wrong in that particular instance. But the fact that we have never had to go back on a single global supplier who is now a BOC supplier because of a SESPA score is a fairly good one-line measure that it is actually working.'

LEGAL OUTSOURCING

SESPA was used by BOC Gases Australia to outsource its legal services to Middletons Moore and Bevins. The Australian legal firm had to satisfy BOC on thirty-four separate attributes. 'By using the SESPA process we were able to focus upon key qualities and capabilities rather than relying on subjective opinions formed during interviews and negotiations,' says David Voet, BOC Gases Australia's group manager, legal services.

The evaluation process began with a cross-functional team

defining the thirty-two separate criteria deemed important for such a supplier. These included responsiveness, market knowledge, communications, use of technology and competency in particular legal fields. 'Interestingly, the SESPA process did not consider price as the key factor in the evaluation,' Voet adds. 'In fact, only four of the thirty-two competencies identified refer to price. This ensures that the decision is based on our total needs.'

'It is a major milestone for us to win the BOC account, particularly following such a thorough process,' says Ian Wilson, chief executive officer of the legal firm which has forty partners and 272 lawyers and support staff. 'BOC Gases was particularly impressed by our firm's commercial approach and the ability to manage corporate accounts.'

TRAVEL OUTSOURCING

BOC also used SESPA when it decided to outsource its global travel arrangements. Its managers and specialist staff around the world travel a total of 100 million miles a year. It is the company's tenth largest item of spend and BOC came to realize that there were some substantial gains to be made from consolidating the services of numerous travel agents around the world into a single global organization. After a lengthy selection procedure, involving SESPA, it outsourced the lion's share of its travel services worldwide to Rosenbluth International. It was believed to be the first global contract of its kind in the world.

It reduced the more than 100 travel agents in sixty different countries BOC had previously been employing to just one global supplier handling over 90 per cent of the company's travel. BOC used the SESPA model to measure travel agents' responses in a rigorous, structured and objective manner, removing individual bias and streamlining the process. 'The competencies we measured included the ability to capture information, global coverage, control of operations and approach to training. And, of course, safety and security featured highly among some thirty attributes scored,' says Lardner.

Pam Koles, BOC's global travel supplier account manager, observes: 'We identified four key spend areas for review – travel management services, air travel, car hire and hotels. With £40 million a year currently being spent on travel-related services, choosing the best company to manage our overall programme is central to the success of the total project.'

Apart from cost benefits, the agreement included a 24-hour global help desk for BOC travellers and it was agreed to set up an on-line reservation system via the Internet. In the first year of operation the global consolidation, plus preferential pricing agreements with leading airline, car hire and hotel companies, saved BOC £3 million in costs.

As important as the cost savings to BOC was the ability to obtain vital data from a single source about the travelling trends of its managers and staff. 'That meant that when we had to negotiate with other travel suppliers, such as airlines and car hire companies, we had from Rosenbluth the necessary management data consolidated from around the world to be able to arrive at the best possible deals. Before it had involved a certain amount of guess work,' says Nicholas Bewes, a member of BOC's travel services supply management team.

Bewes maintains that the rationale behind outsourcing travel services is similar to that applying to other non-core functions: 'I believe there is a growing realization, not only in our company, that there are a lot of suppliers out there who spend millions of pounds investing in becoming good at a particular field of activity that we will never have any interest in becoming good at. A lot of companies see the sense of focusing their resources on what they know well and letting others manage those areas that they do well, working in a partnership. It's the same with us. We need to travel to serve our customers, but we are not a travel company.'

As Peter Varley points out in an article in the 18 September,

1997 issue of *Supply Management* magazine, the consolidation of numerous agencies into a single global organization offers potentially substantial rewards for international organizations – financial, and in terms of service and the provision of accurate and consolidated travel expenditure and activity data. The argument in favour of rationalization also extends to the consolidation of air travel, hotels and car rental services. However, the failure to sell the idea to local management can be the downfall of attempts to rationalize the supply base, no matter how logical the arguments in favour.

Bewes admits there have been the expected growing pains in convincing BOC's managers worldwide that a global outsourcing agreement is to everybody's benefit. Managers are naturally reluctant to give up the established relationships they have with local travel agents, who, they argue, have been providing a personal service for years. Bewes points out that such managers need to be persuaded that minor personal inconvenience can result in major benefits for the group as a whole. It is part of an evolving globalization process that BOC has been undergoing for several years.

This natural resistance can be greatly reduced by involving a cross-section of regular travellers in the decision-making process. BOC, for example, surveyed some 300 of its managers about their travelling preferences before forging a special relationship with a leading airline. It also regularly surveys its most frequent travellers to confirm that Rosenbluth is providing the kind of service that fully meets expectations.

Peter Varley, in his *Supply Management* magazine article, suggests that for companies with a substantial travel budget – say £1 million to £2 million or more – an on-site branch of the travel agent, known as an implant, can provide a high level of service, with operating staff who combine knowledge of company requirements with up-to-the-minute information on new travel products and deals. However, the cost of providing space for the implant must be balanced against the benefit of travellers having convenient and face-to-face access to professional travel advisers, he points out.

IT OUTSOURCING

A report by Andersen Consulting, *Vision 2010: Designing Tomorrow's Organization*, maintains that information technology and telecommunications are the two functions most outsourced. Organizations are willing to hive off any IT activity, from payroll to Internet and intranet services, as long as it is not considered to support a core function crucial to the organization's strategic planning.

The IT outsourcing market in the UK is the largest in Europe. Estimated to be worth more than £2.3 billion, it grew by 38 per cent in 1996 and has expanded by around 40 per cent annually in the past four years. It is eclipsed only by the US, where more than £13.3 billion-worth of contracts were signed in 1995. Everyone seems to have leaped on the IT outsourcing bandwagon, from big names such as ICI, the RAC and Rolls-Royce to government departments, including the DSS and Inland Revenue and local authorities. Analysts expect the UK market for IT outsourcing to be worth £4.8 billion by 2000. However, despite the fact that more organizations are signing up for the first time for IT outsourcing (91 in 1996 compared with 73 in 1995), the rate of growth in value is slowing to an estimated 20 per cent a year, partly due to a shortage of deals in excess of £20 million.

According to an article by Geoff Tyler in the 30 October, 1997 issue of *Supply Management* magazine, companies are also adopting a more selective approach in their outsourcing of IT. Tyler quotes John Lane, of consultancy Pagoda, who says: 'Ownership of PCs and networks is retained, as are user staff, but management and support are outsourced. PCs on site, linked to an outsourced data centre, is becoming a common architecture.'

Tyler cites Birmingham City Council as an example of an

organization that has taken this route. 'Its contractor, ITnet, implemented, and now runs, the housing department network which the council continues to own. But it is not merely about cranking the handle and meeting service-level agreements. ITnet has to keep the client aware of new and emerging technologies.'

According to an article by Sharon Smith in a May 1997 outsourcing supplement published by the *Daily Telegraph*, IT outsourcing is also undergoing a sea-change, from which major trends are emerging. Increasingly, writes Smith, corporations are signing global deals and opting for supplier alliances instead of choosing a single vendor for all their needs.

Part of the change, suggests Smith, is driven by the increasingly global nature of the market. The Pinnacle Alliance, under which JP Morgan outsourced much of its global IT to a consortium consisting of Computer Sciences Corporation, Andersen Consulting, AT&T and Bell Atlantic in a seven-year, £1.25 billion contract in July 1996, is viewed as a prime example of the shift towards alliance and global deals. Analyst Richard Holway says: 'By far the best way of outsourcing is to divide and conquer, because by appointing a number of suppliers a user can play them off against one another for the best deal.'

However, by their very nature, alliances are forcing a seismic shift in commercial behaviour. Paul Burgess, partner at Andersen Consulting, says: 'The consequences of this trend are that companies which traditionally compete with one another are now having to work with each other.'

Users are also opting for several suppliers in separate deals. ICI has outsourced main frame computing services to Origin, its telecommunications networks to Racal and a major part of IT, voice and infrastructure services in Europe to IBM. Such arrangements let ICI avail itself of the specialist skills of each supplier. However, points out Smith, the emerging global focus necessitated by corporates' multinational status is a double-edged sword. Suppliers with the resources to establish a global presence are few and far between. Burgess says: 'Users want a big supplier with an established presence across the world who they know will still be in business in ten years' time. But that does limit consumer choice.'

BP EXPLORATION

In its research to arrive at the best formula to suit its IT outsourcing aims, BP Exploration visited a number of organizations that were outsourcing most, if not all, of their IT to a single supplier and quickly decided that it did not want to follow suit. 'Although a single supplier could provide a seamless package of services and thereby free us from managing the pieces, such an arrangement posed other problems we wished to avoid,' recalls John Cross, head of IT for The British Petroleum Company. 'When a company cedes control of IT to a single provider, it becomes dependent on the quality of the supplier's skills, management, technology and service know-how. In today's dynamic IT services market, no one company can excel in all these areas. Linking its destiny to a single supplier prevents a company from taking advantage of the many innovative, high-quality technologies and services offered by others in the market. Worse, a supplier's capabilities may wane over the life of a contract as its competitors' wax.'

BP Exploration looked for an alternative that would combine the flexibility and control of selective outsourcing with the comprehensive service offered by a single provider. 'We knew we did not want to lock ourselves into long-term contracts with our outsourcing partners,' Cross wrote in a *Harvard Business Review* article. 'A couple of companies we visited had signed ten-year contracts with their suppliers, essentially freezing the companies into technology solutions that were no longer meeting the needs of their changing businesses.'

Before arriving at the best balance to meet its needs, BP Exploration first had to get its own house in order. To improve service and reduce the cost of duplicated systems incurred through acquisitions, it consolidated seven IT departments into a single global IT department with centralized financial control. It then standardized systems across the company.

When it started to examine the market of IT service providers, it seriously considered any interested provider. Because it was certain it would hire more than one contractor, it did not need to limit its search to companies that could provide a full array of IT services. At the end of 1991, it mailed 100 requests for information packets to large and small providers. The request for information outlined the company's intention to re-focus its IT department and summarized the scope of the work it intended to outsource. It gleaned responses from sixty-five potential service providers, thus gaining a wealth of information about the market for IT services – in particular, the strengths and weaknesses of all major and most minor players. Through discussions, it whittled the list down to sixteen US and European companies.

Senior IT managers from BP Exploration closely examined each of the contender's management staff and culture, the depth of its understanding about the outsourcing industry and its strategic vision. Eventually the sixteen potential providers were reduced to a shortlist of six. Rather than providing these front-runners with a detailed description of BP's specifications for fulfilling the outsourcing task, it decided to ask the outsourcers themselves to come up with a plan to provide a seamless service that would enable the winners of the contract to work together. All six suppliers were invited to week-long interactive workshops and were given the task of creating an alliance composed of more than one supplier but fewer than five to meet BP's specifications. This meant that they devised solutions to meet BP's needs among themselves and took responsibility for providing the services.

The proposal BP eventually accepted, submitted by Sema Group, Science Applications International Corporation and Syncordia (a subsidiary of British Telecommunications that subsequently became part of Concert, a joint venture between

BT and MCI), met all its expectations. Unlike other proposals, these three companies were able to show how they genuinely complemented each other.

Business managers at each of BP Exploration's eight major sites negotiated with the company's IT suppliers for customized services. The similar framework agreements between each provider and BP Exploration defined the generic services provided, the legal provisions, the general commercial principles of financial targets, margins and incentives, quality assurance, performance reviews and a host of other issues across the company. Working within these framework agreements, each site negotiated its own contracts, specifying the scope of services, service levels and performance targets. At some sites, the BP management team negotiated only with the primary provider for delivery of all services.

LOGISTICS OUTSOURCING

Anyone who regularly travels the motorways of the UK will be familiar with the brand names of the major transport firms. They are blazoned on the sides of the huge vehicles that invariably block your view of the next road sign. Companies planning to outsource their logistics for the first time are quite likely to be tempted to opt for one of these familiar names, but in the view of Denis O'Sullivan, the IBM transformation management consultant, that is not always the right decision. 'A lot of companies – particularly the smaller ones – get carried away by the big brand names. They don't know where else to turn. The problem is they may be in a niche business. Therefore, they will need to find a niche supplier who actually knows their business and the areas in which they operate. It can be difficult.'

Perhaps surprisingly, companies have not been very successful in developing sophisticated IT systems to schedule and manage their transportation fleets. It has therefore fallen on the third-party logistics firms to face up to this challenge. Because of the complexity of the task the third-party logistics firms are themselves turning to outside IT firms to help them come up with appropriate systems. In other words, the outsourcer providers are outsourcing themselves.

Major retailers like Sainsbury's, Tesco and Asda are investing vast sums in transport planning which they are using to manage both their in-house operations and their third-party operations. They outsource a significant part of logistics, but they retain management control.

Newcomers to logistics outsourcing are probably best advised either to seek the advice of specialist consultants or benchmark companies in similar fields of activity which have long experience of using third-party services. O'Sullivan suggests that newcomers should try to track down logistics firms who have an established reputation for serving customers with similar products. 'You don't want to be a test bed for a logistic company that thinks this is a good niche market to get into,' he stresses. 'Talk to your customers and ask them to recommend third-party operators who are acting on behalf of their suppliers and are actually providing a good service. If they mention a third-party logistics firm that constantly lets them down, you will know that is one to avoid.

'Always get competitive quotes. Always think through the service levels you should be achieving in your business and not the ones you are achieving. Most importantly, think of the way your business may change in the next five years.'

O'Sullivan also warns that newcomers to outsourcing should be cautious about the nature of the contract they are signing. 'Don't automatically sign off the contract that is presented by the service provider. It's very important to involve people who understand the business issues in the contract. It's only a legal document if the contract breaks down. Until then it is an operational document. It is important to make sure the right measures are contained in it. As in any outsourcing agreement, it should cover what you are looking to achieve in the business, what the customer service levels are, the information you expect to receive. It should be remembered that you're not outsourcing today's business, you are outsourcing tomorrow's business.'

Experts will say it is ill-advised for a company to hand over all of its logistics assets in case things don't work out and it proves necessary to pull the operation back in-house. That could end up with the company finding itself in square one again and having to make a lot of fresh capital investments. However, O'Sullivan points out that it won't make economic sense for a small company with a fleet of five or ten vehicles, say, and a small warehouse operation to continue maintaining those facilities once it has taken the outsourcing route. Larger retailers, on the other hand, play safe and often only outsource part of their operations so that they still have some resources to fall back on in an emergency. Also, by retaining a distribution fleet in some regions of the country they have a benchmark with which to compare the services provided by the third-party logistics firm. At the same time it encourages the third-party provider to maintain high performance standards in the hope that it will eventually win all of the business.

O'Sullivan warns that companies that go into partnership with third-party logistics providers should realize that they are about to take part in a totally new ball-game that requires a change of mind-set. 'You have companies talking about establishing partnerships with their suppliers without actually realizing that it is a totally different sort of business. Almost the only people not directly affected in terms of what he or she should be doing are the chief executive and chairman. Below them, everyone is affected. The buyers who used to be told: "Go out and kick your suppliers," are now being told: "Be good to them and work together with them." It's a whole new world.'

CLEANING CONTRACTS

Cleanliness in the food-processing industry, as Geoff Tyler points out in an article in *Supply Management* magazine, is little short of a religion. It is also a faith policed by government inspectors and by the even more fearsome inspectors of the major supermarket chains. Tyler cites the example of Grimsby-based Coldwater Seafoods. When Jeff Crowther, the company's production director, decided to outsource the cleaning operations of the company's food-processing plant, the exercise was clearly going to be exacting. Coldwater is one of the largest suppliers of supermarket branded seafood products and has a position well worth guarding.

Adds Tyler: 'Cleaning at the original plant and a recently-acquired expansion plant was originally carried out by in-house teams. Outsourcing the cleaning was part of a larger core activity analysis which also resulted in contracting out cold storage, distribution, catering and security.

'Cleaning was selected for outsourcing for operational reasons. Crowther explains that occasional priority clashes could arise, with the cleaning team reporting to the manufacturing management which also had responsibility for hygiene management. The outsourcing contractor, therefore, would be taking on the role of hygiene manager, albeit subject to client-side participation and inspections. Cost was not an issue, although a small cost-saving has been achieved. The requirement was for a thorough strip down of the processing lines, cleaning and re-assembly overnight between the daily sixteen hours of production shifts – from 10 pm to about 6 am in fact.'

Crowther told Tyler: 'We had an existing hygiene programme, which we used for tender comparison purposes. But once we had made our choice – Initial Foodguard – we worked with them on improvements to it, listened to their expertise on working practices plus the benefits of new materials of which they had an experience and we had not.'

Tyler's article takes up the story again: 'One important innovation at the time was the use of ATP rapid bacteria monitoring. Traditional swabs require some 48 hours to grow a culture for examination, but ATP chemical analysis gives a readout from swabs in minutes – quick enough to take any corrective action there and then.

'Once the new programme was agreed, including which products and methods Initial would introduce, the management structure was decided. Initial takes over the lines at the end of the day and Coldwater does not accept them back until the cleaning has been inspected, readings taken and the results recorded by a management duo from Initial and Coldwater. The principle, says Crowther, actually makes quality management easier and more secure.'

Andrew Manning, a consultant with facilities management company FM2, maintains that the quality trend in outsourced cleaning is contractor-led. 'Outsourced cleaning is still looked upon by too many purchasing executives as a commodity purchase and they are still tending to buy on price, often at the expense of quality. Contractors recognize this and the harm it can do to both clients' standards and their own industry, and are turning their marketing towards value-added services and quality management. Sales promises include such things as better supervision and use of new high-tech cleaning systems. At FM2 we also seek detailed assurance on how the contractor will manage the contract and the people operating it – for example, we want to know details of the incentives that will be given to do a conscientious job.'

The British Cleaning Council warns purchasing executives who are evaluating tenders to do so with the help of a knowledgeable mind. It can cite many examples of how unforeseen needs, resulting from inexpert tender specification, can allow the unscrupulous operator to quote a low price and earn expensive extras later. Initial protection of hard floors to reduce refurbishment work, removal of limescale in kitchens and washrooms as well as orthodox cleaning, and using battery-powered machines where mains cables will become a safety hazard are among the issues.

The Cleaning & Support Services Association offers to help purchasing executives in drawing up a cleaning contract specification and publishes its Code of Practice to which member firms are expected to adhere. It also has a quick-glance guide to evaluating tenders:

- Do staff levels seem realistic?
- Is the level of supervisors to cleaners adequate?
- Is pay realistic?
- Is insurance cover adequate?
- Are provisions made for staff training?
- How often will the area manager visit your contract?

SECURITY

On the face of it, an organization's security is a typical non-core function that is ripe for outsourcing. Indeed, when would-be entrepreneurs first start their infant commercial ventures, the serviced office accommodation they commonly use comes complete with security systems and perhaps security staff as part of the outsourced package.

Yet there are very few examples of totally outsourced security functions in the UK and Europe and where outsourcing is practised it invariably involves the use of a managing consultant or some other intermediary. Research conducted for this book failed to find any example of a total security function outsourced directly to a security services/systems provider. Why this is so requires both an analysis of the nature of the security function and a brief history of the security industry itself.

The term security conjures up a picture of burglar alarms, closed-circuit television systems and security guards in ever more imposing uniforms. That is the immediately visible face of security, widely known as premises security. Of course, the modern organization has many more security needs than that. IT security involves data back-up, communications integrity measures and disaster recovery contingencies. Staff may need training to deal effectively with dangerous incidents, especially in any form of retail or field-work situation. Internal investigations into suspected fraud, due diligence measures, business intelligence projects and employee vetting are all part of the security mix. In addition, executives may need personal protection and education in how to avoid the risks of, say, kidnap or ransom, especially while travelling or working abroad.

All these aspects of the security mix impinge to a greater or lesser degree on issues that are of a confidential nature and which, if handled without discretion, can cause an organization embarrassment or a poor public relations image. Companies that use animals in medical research, for example, have to take special measures to guard against infiltration by animal rights protesters. This will almost certainly require more than the usual site perimeter security and calls for especially careful vetting of job applicants.

The sensitive nature of security does not have to be as dramatic as that, however. Clothing companies, for instance, need to guard new designs until they appear on the catwalk before retail buyers. No company wants its research and design unit infiltrated – mere vandalism and common theft are the least of concerns in such cases.

Apprehensions

Not surprisingly, therefore, the use of outsiders to maintain critical security measures is accompanied by all manner of apprehensions. That alone would not be an insurmountable barrier to security outsourcing if the security industry was capable of demonstrating an ability to allay those apprehensions. Sadly, most of its customers do not believe that to be the case – a lack of faith that owes as much to historic problems as to current ones.

The security industry has two very different components. Alarm and surveillance technology is first-class – indeed much of it is a spin-off from systems researched for military use. Initial problems arising from the poor standards of companies which specified and installed those systems are now largely, though not entirely, overcome by the inspection efforts of organizations like NACOSS – the National Approval Council for Security Systems – and by alarm control centres through which verification of alarm calls can be made such that police will actually attend.

Guarding companies, in contrast, have a bad reputation for poor quality of service. Quality maintenance measures by the Inspectorate of the Security Industry have gone a long way to improve the situation, though not all quality-conscious guarding contractors subscribe to it, but there are also still many poor quality guarding companies, often operating in only one local area, that are still giving the whole industry a bad name, which in general terms it no longer deserves.

Added to those unfavourable perceptions of the security industry is the fact that, apart from a handful of very large national and international concerns, security companies cannot offer the full spectrum of guarding, alarm systems and surveillance systems, let alone the additional services of internal investigations, IT security, disaster recovery and so on. Some of the top companies offering a wide range of security services are now rising to this challenge, though many others remain based on deeply-rooted single service divisional lines. The challenge is being taken up because organizations have shown the security industry ample evidence that they are ready to outsource the security function provided a competent contractor can be found to take it on.

The benefits perceived by companies in outsourcing security revolve around the familiar ones of lower overall costs, due in part to cost-sharing, coupled with enjoying a better security operation due to security specialists' greater access to, and use of, expertise.

Part of the deal

The premises–related aspects of security – buildings alarm systems, CCTV, security guards, receptionists – are commonly included in the package of functions outsourced to facilities management contractors along with cleaning, maintenance, staff restaurant, mailroom and so on. The accompanying IT–related security measures are commonly included in IT outsourcing operations. The area of disaster recovery – provision of standby office accommodation and IT systems – may be appended to either.

Geoff Tyler, writing in *Security Management Today* magazine's August 1998 issue, found from research among leading facilities management contractors such as Symonds Group, Care Services and Integral that security is more often part of the contract than not. Tyler notes that clients of Symonds Group, such as Blue Water Retail Centre in Kent, British Standards Institution and BP–Mobil, already include the security brief in the facilities they outsource to the services provider.

'There is no logic in excluding security,' Julian Darwell-Stone, a director of Symonds Group, told Tyler. 'Cross-skilling opportunities may exist, for example where security staff are required to undertake administrative duties such as mail-sorting during closed hours, when their management in both roles will be the responsibility of the facilities management operator. Usually the whole security operation and its manager report to the facilities manager, a Symonds employee. Only in certain environments like banking, where security may include activities related to the core business, will the function report to a core business manager.'

The government's Private Finance Initiative aims to outsource to the private sector the provision of premises within which public sector activities take place. Government offices and hospitals are two obvious examples. The private sector provision of such premises includes the total security needs for the duration of their occupation under the PFI arrangement.

Consultancy provision

Another focus through which security is outsourced is the consultancy area. Though security consultants and risk assessment companies do not provide security measures as such, they do possess the ability to advise on issues right across the security spectrum. This is in contrast to the fragmentation of the security industry itself and has arisen, arguably, as an antidote to that fragmentation. Often the consultancy will put in place a temporary security manager whose role is to manage the re-engineering or fresh creation of the security function, using such contractors as he or she, under the consultancy's direction, deems fit. That manager will remain in place at least until the implementation is complete and capable of being run on its own momentum. Then, however, the consultancy invariably headhunts a permanent security manager and hands the operation over to the client.

In a very few cases, security consultants have evolved into an outsourcing role. Tyler cited in his article the example of Paul Elliott Consultancy which acts as the security manager for such organizations as B&Q, House of Fraser and several major banks. The consultancy literally runs its clients' security functions, as Elliott explains:

'Typically I report to my client's board of directors and they expect my people to align their security function to best practice and keep them appraised of performance. That includes the full spectrum of premises security systems, shrinkage (petty theft) and similar internal investigations, store detectives, guarding and security audits. I am responsible for choosing which security services the client needs to use from the security industry and profession.'

The examples cited above involve outsourcing the security function not to a security services provider but to a facilities management operation, PFI or similar contractor or via the management services of a consultant. It is, nevertheless, true outsourcing from the client's perspective. There is no security manager as such left within the client organization. There will be a security outsourcing management function, of course, but this may well be undertaken by a board member or senior manager in a supervisory role, probably alongside other managerial duties. Indeed, because of the emphasis now placed on assessing the quality of service provided under a service level agreement, the 'security manager' may well be a senior member of the buying department. Whoever it is, that person is the one to whom the watching brief has been assigned; it will not be that person's role to co-ordinate the various elements of the security requirement – guarding, alarm systems, surveillance, investigations and so on, nor to formulate security management decisions in detail. That should be done by the outsourcing contractor according to the terms of the outsourcing agreement.

The nearest example of a security function being outsourced directly that Tyler could find involved Coopers & Lybrand (now known as PricewaterhouseCoopers), the accountancy firm. National security manager Mark Rayburn has just two other security people on the Coopers & Lybrand payroll – a regional manager and a London manager. Security managers at the individual company locations are employed by Securicor and have the normal management responsibility for their own teams of officers. They also have upward responsibility to Rayburn just as if they were on the payroll. Site instructions are written by the Securicor manager, submitted to Coopers & Lybrand for approval and implemented by Securicor managers without further reference. Rayburn assesses quality of performance, of course, but the principle is no different from having an in-house team.

However, that is only the guarding element of the security function. Other aspects are handled by other contractors or in-house at Coopers & Lybrand. Enquiries among security contractors reveal that what many claim to be an outsourcing contract in fact boils down to contracting out the security guarding operations along with part of the day-to-day management structure (usually supervisory level). Many other claiming outsourced assignments were not even providing this, but simply offered a guarding service on a sole contractor basis. The decision on alarm and surveillance systems, internal investigations and, most of all, budget spending, rested with the client company.

More comprehensive service

Somewhat belatedly, some security companies, able to offer a more comprehensive than average range of services, are at last making strategic moves to respond to the growing desire of client companies to outsource the whole security operation as a non-core activity. The promise of a sea-change is as yet only a ripple, but it is likely to gather momentum in the years ahead. The biggest single obstacle these companies have is to convince their would-be clients of their capabilities.

Some of the impetus comes from America where security companies have been seeking true outsource business in recent years with, so far, only limited success. There, the move is being led by those security firms in the forefront of guarding services, but these contractors are re-organizing internally to ensure that there are no barriers between their specialized functions which could impede a thorough, seamless, service.

In the UK, security companies have a greater degree of re-organizing to do than in the US. Here, virtually all security companies have grown from one root such as guarding services and have added systems installation and investigatory work and so on, usually as a result of mergers and acquisitions. The tendency has been for those services to continue operating as discrete marketing activities.

That said, several UK companies are undergoing the necessary re-organization to offer a more comprehensive service, identifying their strengths and weaknesses and addressing them either by internal re-appraisals or by further mergers with companies that have complementary assets. This will enable clients to go for the one-stop-shop approach, rather than employing consultants or other intermediaries to trawl the market and select the best offerings from many different suppliers.

There is, of course, no reason why an outsourcing contractor should not in turn sub-contract specialised areas to other firms. In theory the client should be unconcerned as to the source of the service as long as it is operated efficiently. In practice, client companies like to know that the contractor is capable of providing from its own resources all those activities which the client regards as central to the security function. So if, for example, executive protection is only occasionally needed – perhaps when someone travels to a high-risk part of the world – then sub-contracting will be acceptable. However, if protection is required every day, the client is likely to want to know that it will be provided by people working seamlessly with the premises security team.

The remaining issue is the reluctance, at security manager level, to entertain outsourcing. This is due in part to the problems described above and which the industry is beginning to address. It is also due in part to the usual fears of loss of job and/or status. Reluctance is, however, by no means universal. All security companies can name senior managers and even directors among their ranks who began their careers in client company security teams, saw little prospect of promotion and were delighted to transfer to a specialist security company where they could aspire to the managing director's job. Security outsourcing's limited progress so far is the only reason why this career advantage is not as well appreciated in security circles as it is in, say, IT circles.

SUMMARY

From the above overview, it is clear that there is a broad range of options that companies can adopt when deciding to take the outsourcing route. For example, BOC favours single-source providers that can meet all its needs, apart from those retained in-house. Where, in the case of the outsourced legal services, that single provider cannot be expected to cover the full range of services in every geographic location, the provider itself is left to solve the problem by appointing affiliates to cover the weak spots. BP Exploration, on the other hand, was anxious, when it decided to outsource its IT facilities, not to depend on a single provider, believing that no single contractor could meet all its needs. Instead, it invited an alliance of potential contractors to come up with a plan themselves in which their complementary skills covered all BP's needs.

It cannot be denied that there are risks attached to opting for single-source providers. Even the most-established contractors can expect to run into problems from time to time. A case in point is EDS, the world's largest IT services firm, which experienced difficulties at the beginning of 1998 with the installation of a new system called European Administration Resources System (Ears). As a result of the temporary failure of the system, bailiffs visited the European headquarters of EDS at Stockley Park in Middlesex demanding the payment of an outstanding bill. According to an article in *Computer Week*, the glitches in the computer system resulted in piles of unpaid bills and a number of legal actions by creditors.

This was something of an embarrassment to EDS, a Texan firm founded by the aspiring US presidential candidate H. Ross Perot, and which had been awarded the £1.5 billion contract to take charge of the information technology systems for the Inland Revenue, including the processing of all the tax forms for the controversial switch to self-assessment. EDS has also won contracts for the Department of Social Security, the Department of Transport and the London Borough of Brent and handles more government outsourcing than any other firm. The failure of one of its own systems added fuel to criticisms that too much government outsourcing had been handed over to a single IT provider.

There are obviously arguments for and against multiple suppliers that can give rise to endless debate. At the end of the day, outsourcers have to make a decision for themselves and learn from hard experience. In the view of Bob Aylott, head of KPMG's outsourcing advisory service, the decision to go for multiple suppliers doesn't reduce the risks, 'because each supplier is expert in one domain and each domain in itself is a risk – so maybe you widen the risk. The other aspect is that most of the components into which an outsourced function is broken up is part of a service delivery chain in practice. Each component has some inter-dependency and therefore it requires some co-operation at quite a detailed working level between the suppliers.'

Getting a number of suppliers to create their own plan of how they will co-operate together is fine in principle, suggests Aylott, but he argues that it is unlikely to work in practice because there is little incentive for the members of the alliance to work together. There may be a strong argument in favour of the idea of best-in-class providers of discrete parts of an outsourced operation who forge a close relationship and understanding of each other as the alliance develops, but the case against multiple suppliers, in Aylott's view, is that it is difficult to maintain multiple relationships. If there are two suppliers of similar services they will be reluctant to expose innovative ideas in case they are acquired by the other partner.

Also, however much the members of the alliance try to co-operate, there will always be a prevailing competitive instinct that will compel them to try to outshine each other in the eyes of the client. 'There are a lot of problems that have to be balanced against the best-in-class model,' says Aylott. 'My preference is to have a prime contractor and the others working through that prime provider. The affiliates need not be selected by the prime provider.

'There are other aspects when you consider multiple suppliers. They place a multiple obligation on the internal organization to manage at a detailed level. One of the aspects the function being outsourced fights against is losing control. What very often is meant by that is operational control. By fragmenting it among many suppliers they outsource it at the middle of the spider's web of control. They tend to manage the process, while outsourcing really ought to be about managing the outcomes.'

Similarly, as the case studies in this chapter illustrate, there is a lot of debate about the ideal length of an outsourced contract. BOC's Craig Lardner is of the view that once the best provider has been found, the contract should be long-term – ideally for ever. His argument is that BOC and the supplier should work in partnership to iron out any shortcomings that arise. BP Exploration, on the other hand, negotiates new performance contracts with its IT suppliers on a regular basis (usually for five-year periods), believing that new technologies and operating methods are constantly changing and require continual reviewing.

John Cross of BP would argue that in an ideal world indefinite contracts are an admirable goal, but practice has taught him otherwise. 'I regard myself as wanting to be a creature of the market place and I have found in the long run that if you make decisions that fundamentally buck the realities of what's going on in the market place, you're in trouble. Therefore, the statement of love and loyalty to your partners is very fine, but if your partner does not in fact become a best-in-class service organization in the fullness of time because others come round on the inside track and become better, then you aren't actually doing your business any ultimate favours – unless you think you have the capability to influence and change that supplier so that it retains its leading-edge position.

'My feeling is that this whole service industry, which represents tens of billions of dollars now, is still far from settled. It's still in fragments. I think the players will go on forming and re-forming and you want at least to have the opportunity to be able to float on the market's best opportunities when they occur with a degree of certainty for your supplier, so that the investment they're going to make in you and the relationship is going to have a reasonable payback for them and I guess most of them think five years is about right.'

Cross believes shorter-term contracts are particularly relevant when offering contracts to small outsourcing organizations. In the early days BP selected a very small IT service provider in the US, which was eventually taken over by Wang. 'Wang has got a very different strategy and view on the world. That taught us a lesson that even though small, smart organizations can be very tempting because they can be very agile and dynamic, they are at the same time very vulnerable. A take-over can alter radically the strategy of the organization if you're not careful.'

Practically all outsourcing experts agree that companies planning to hand over operations to a third party should first get their own house in order. Companies should not outsource because they want to get rid of a problem that they haven't taken the time and trouble to sort out for themselves. They should hand over a well-run operation, whatever function it is performing, to a third-party provider that can do an even better job. BP Exploration, for example, first made sure that it had rationalized the rag-bag of IT operations it had inherited through a series of acquisitions before it sought an alliance of contractors to run the operation as a seamless efficient service.

The most important issue, in Bob Aylott's view, is not to lose sight of the objectives of an outsourcing arrangement. 'You've got to keep coming back to them because people forget them or they learn things which actually change their objectives,' he says. 'The second step is to document what exists at the moment, whether it's service level agreements, people skills or whatever. It's a sort of inventory stage. The next stage is finding suppliers with whom you are prepared to do business – pinning down the market and distinguishing between those who theoretically could do the job and those you would be happy to deal with because of their track record, credibility, financial acumen, whatever it may be. You are then into producing invitations to tender or some equivalent document against which suppliers can bid competitively.'

Denis O'Sullivan of IBM stresses that it is important that outsourcing should not be looked at in isolation. 'You have to do it in the context of your total business and where you are going tomorrow. That's where people get it wrong. If, when outsourcing any function, you just look to get the cheapest possible price, you will get value for the money you pay. If you really want value you should be prepared to pay extra for that value. Too many companies aren't prepared to do that. Finally, don't outsource a problem; outsource a solution – something that is running as efficiently as you can get it. There will be more work in achieving that, but it will bring far greater benefits.'

6
Monitoring the Contract

The greatest fear managers have when considering outsourcing is losing control, particularly of functions critical to the survival of the organization. Warns Dr Michael Hunt, managing director of AKZO Nobel Chemicals: 'In practice outsourcing is similar to delegation. You must have good reporting systems and tight control of costs.'

Echoes David Turnbull, chief executive of the UK 200 Group of Practising Chartered Accountants: 'It is an innovative management tool which works best when closely monitored. We see it from both angles. Accountancy firms of all sizes are having more work outsourced to them – and this will grow.'

The UK 200 Group, with a membership of about 180 established independent practices throughout the UK, itself outsources a number of central services including publishing, training and promotional activities. 'It can be very effective,' says Turnbull, 'if you don't lose control. You've got to have a clear reporting structure.'

Spoiled garden

The unfortunate consequences that can result from a failure of communication between a company and its contractors was graphically illustrated in a 1997 *Western Morning News* article written by Nick Constable:

It was a shady Westcountry garden, tucked beside one of Britain's most beautiful rural railways. For owners Lewis and Lynette Davey the onset of spring was eagerly awaited. The much-loved lilac and mock-orange syringa trees bordering their lawn were due to blossom – just as they had for the previous 19 years. Then, without warning, the maintenance men of Railtrack Great Western moved in.

Mrs Davey was woken in the early hours by a thundering roar and the sound of crashing timber from the line below. She rushed from her bed in time to see a huge rotary trimming blade, carried on a floodlit yellow locomotive crane, scythe neatly through her 15 ft trees. There was no time to stop the crew – even if she had braved the blizzard of timber shards showering on to her lawn. Within ten seconds the entire hedgerow was reduced to uniform five-feet-high bare stalks.

The Daveys, both 65, of Railway Cottages, Lapford, Devon, are still seething at Railtrack's blunder. They believe the damage could take years to repair and say the company's offer of financial compensation is no substitute for the shade and beauty of their beloved trees. The garden forms a boundary with Railtrack's Tarka Line – a 40-mile link between Exeter and Barnstaple winding through countryside enshrined in Henry Williamson's classic novel, *Tarka the Otter*.

Because of a steep embankment, the couple say it would be impossible to plant mature trees in the spot. Mrs Davey said: 'I still can't quite believe what has happened. One minute we were lying in our beds; the next we heard a horrendous noise and saw the giant flail levelling our garden. The train just carried on into the night.' She said the track was cut back every year and maintenance workers were usually careful to trim only overhanging branches. The destruction of the syringa had ruined the view from the 160-year-old cottage and would leave the couple nowhere to string their hammock.

A Railtrack spokesman said: 'We have apologized and we will consider any reasonable claim for compensation. The contractors responsible have sent a team to clear up the mess in the garden.'

When responsibilities are passed down the line to a third party, misunderstandings will inevitably occur – although one would hope with less dire consequences than those related above – but it is impossible to legislate for every eventuality. However, outsourcing – like delegation – does not mean abdicating total responsibility. The day-to-day worry may be taken off your hands, but the ultimate responsibility still rests with the outsourcing organization. At the end of the day, a company's customers will not want to know who specifically is to blame for a failed delivery or a faulty product. The customer will simply reassess its opinion of the provider, regardless of who actually caused the foul-up.

Ongoing relationship

But once a company has drawn up a contract with a third-party provider, how should it manage the ongoing relationship? Obviously the company's expectations will be based on what it hoped to achieve when it first drew up the outsourcing agreement. One way of monitoring progress is to go back and re-visit the original objectives to see if they are on track. Have you changed your objectives since you outsourced? Are you now getting more or less than you thought originally?

You can outsource, but you can't walk away. You can't walk away from the people who are managing your IT, for example. If, for whatever reason, what they're delivering doesn't meet the needs of the end-users, simply saying it is no longer your responsibility doesn't solve anything.

Take a hospital, for example. A hospital may decide to outsource its cleaning contracts, but that doesn't mean the hospital no longer has any responsibility for cleanliness. Try telling that to the Health & Safety Inspectorate. Try telling it to the coroner when there is an outbreak of infection. It remains the responsibility of the hospital management. Services are outsourced on an ongoing basis, so that failure to comply with expectations becomes more visible earlier.

To some extent there is a shift in expectations with outsourcing. If IT is supplied internally, after a while the in-house users get used to a fall off in quality – if the systems aren't particularly responsive, for example – and they downgrade their expectations in line with that perception. So they fix things for themselves and they don't allow themselves to become too upset with shortcomings at the centre. When IT is outsourced, on the other hand, it is more likely that expectations will rise – that the outsourcing firm will in time demand more than before. The end-users might want more, but that may not be what the contract specifies. The contract may not specify anything better than the company had before.

So you can't conclude that outsourcing is signed and sealed just because the decision to outsource has been taken. It continues to be an area of review. If it is simply a make or buy decision, the outsourcing company could decide to reverse its decision five years down the track.

Outsourcing companies need to be clear when drawing up a contract what their expectations are. Typically, if you outsource IT, the outsource provider buys up the existing computer hardware. You must write into the contract what you would do if this breaks down. If you take the example of the hospital contract, you may well hand over all the cleaning equipment to the contractor, but what would you do if you ever wanted to in-source it again? You will immediately have quite heavy capital costs, which may well have some bearing on your decision.

Bob Aylott maintains this need not be a problem because a carefully conceived contract can cover such requirements without much difficulty. 'The trouble is a lot of people don't ensure it is in the contract so they are in difficulty, but exit arrangements are relatively straightforward. On the IT side, which is the most documented area, two-thirds of outsourcing agreements are being renewed with the same supplier, one third aren't. Very few are being pulled back in-house. But the same problem applies. You have got to transfer the assets, so whether they come back in or go to another supplier, it's the same problem.'

SERVICE LEVEL AGREEMENTS

The service level agreement drawn up at the contract stage of the outsourcing should provide key guidelines on how to monitor the ongoing relationship between the outsourcing company and the provider. Observes Mike Dodsworth, human resources manager at Cap Gemini, the international IT services provider: 'In terms of ongoing service, the whole thing is geared to a service level agreement and it can be a pretty big document. Obviously, the bigger the deal the more the service level agreement will do, but effectively it's a process of stick and carrot. The service level agreement sets down what you are contracted to deliver. It has penalties in it if you fail to deliver and probably has some encouragement – perhaps one of the objectives is to reduce the IT costs by ten per cent. There may be some benefit-sharing in that.'

Dodsworth stresses that service level *agreement* is the key word. 'It's a document jointly agreed. It's not Cap Gemini saying that's what we are going to do for you or indeed the client saying that's what I want you to do. It has to be agreement and if that document is to live it has to be reviewed every six months at least.

I think the real measure of Cap Gemini's success is that the service level agreement, and the service management process we have around it, is dusted off and looked at a lot. But if the actual contract on which the service level agreement is based has to come out of the drawer, we have failed.'

Aylott of KPMG points out that there are, however, limitations to the aspects that can be covered by a service level agreement: 'Obviously you want to have a contractual framework that places sensible obligations on both parties. The most important part of regular service delivery is to have service level agreements, service reporting against business meaningful measures – physical deliverables. Service level agreements are broadly adequate for a technically-based service, but when you get into a business-oriented service, then one also needs to have business metrics which are not attributable to any single service agreement, but are an amalgamation of the outcome of a lot of things. They may not be totally within the domain of the contract, but certainly significantly influenced by what is in the domain of the contract.'

Aylott cites the example of a retailer/supplier relationship. 'The warehouse picking is controlled by a computer system, but the retail business metric is that they have a 24-hour turnaround on all their pickings. Lots of things can go wrong with the computer system – or go right – and still achieve that, which would be subject to a service level agreement. But the real business metric is that the retailer wants a 24-hour turnaround on everything. If you tie the supplier into that then you are, in a sense, widening their interest outside the computer system to the things which are operational.

'It's like the car companies. People get paid for the number of sprayed cars that go out the door. The spray company has a spray booth on the production line. The cars don't go out the door for all sorts of reasons, one of which could be poor paint quality. Nevertheless, the spray company is tied into the business metric, over which it doesn't have 100 per cent control. It recognizes what that business is about and the fact that everybody should be thinking about that as the objective. That's an uncomfortable position to be in, but increasingly it is something people are prepared to accept.'

Sanction and redress

The outsourcing of areas that are close to the customer raises the issue of what to do when a service provider under-performs. Malcolm Brown, in an article on outsourcing published by *Management Today*, observes: 'The thing about outsourcing is that to the customer, the whole operation is invisible. If the service provider does something that hurts the customer, it isn't the provider who gets it in the neck, it is the company that farmed out that part of its work. The only way to avoid such disasters is to be vigilant before and during the outsourcing, and to make sure that you have sanction and redress; ultimately that you have a way to dismiss the under-performer. The hard-nosed would say that the best way to keep providers up to scratch is to keep them on short-term contracts, constantly aware that under-performance will mean the chop. This flies in the face of more modern supply chain management advocates, however, who would argue that by involving suppliers or sub-contractors closely and building up a relationship of trust, everyone can win.'

The decision on whether to go for a short-term or long-term contract depends on the kind of deal that is being set up, in Aylott's view. 'If it is a commodity deal you're running on an "as is" basis, then the contract doesn't need to be long. It depends on how much effort you want the supplier to put in. If the supplier is to put in a lot of effort, then it needs to recover that effort, because part of the reason is you want to leverage the supplier's investment in the deal for the client's benefit. If you have a short deal the ability to leverage that and to reduce the costs accordingly is not so great. So the length of the deal is really first and foremost a bit of arithmetic, primarily the amount of investment you expect the supplier to make. Some of that will be efficiency type investment, but some of it may be relationship building investment. They're not going to build a relationship and put effort in if it is going to be closed off after three years. So, if you're building a capability type service, that only begins to deliver value after two or three years, it would be stupid to cut it off at that point.'

BOC'S SESPA MODEL

BOC, the UK-based industrial gases group, uses the same criteria it set out to select its outsource provider to monitor service standards. The attributes it requires providers to have can be quite extensive. The most it has ever insisted on is 63 and the least is twenty-seven. In the case of the outsourced legal services in Australia, it required thirty-four criteria to be met. This may seem excessive, but Craig Lardner, BOC's group manager, supply management, is convinced that such thoroughness pays off in spades. For example, one of the questions contained in the request for information at the time of the bidding involved response time. It asked prospective suppliers what they were prepared to commit to by way of response time when a legal inquiry was made. Middletons Moore & Bevins (MMB), the Australian legal firm that ultimately won the contract, committed to a response time of twenty-four hours and a minimum of three pieces of critical information.

The promised information included the legal firm's best estimate of the amount of time it will take to deal with the issue raised; which lawyer it was going to assign to the matter and any conflict of interest. 'We asked for one piece of information and they gave us a promise to come up with the vital issues within twenty-four hours,' says Lardner. 'That means we have a measure in place today between MMB and us as to how many times it doesn't respond within twenty-four hours – and MMB does the measurement itself. It knows when it has got an inquiry and it knows when it is responding.

'What MMB is delighted about is that it has put a process in place to meet that commitment. MMB met with its partners and its lawyers and agreed that if it worked for BOC, all its big corporate clients could be offered exactly the same response time. MMB would just have to put a process in place. Now when that law firm bids for business it offers a 24-hour response time which blows their prospective customer out of the water. Now MMB has a competitive advantage in winning corporate accounts as a direct result of building a process around a promise that came from an attribute from a client that said it really needed commitment to a response time. So we've helped our client grow its business other than just our own business. We've helped MMB improve their process. We now expect this to be part and parcel of BOC's relationship with its suppliers.'

CLEANING CONTRACTS

Office cleaning was one of the first functions to be outsourced. On the surface it would seem a very uncomplicated function to outsource and monitor. Nevertheless sophisticated forms of monitoring have been introduced in recent years that leave little doubt about whether the job is being done according to the terms set out in the outsourcing contract.

The Palace of Westminster cleaning contract involves working on valuable and often delicate interiors, treating materials with respect and adhering to security requirements. Graham Good, senior works directorate manager at Westminster, uses a computer monitoring system when inspecting the cleaning results, 'because if one writes performance into a contract, there has to be a way of measuring that performance accurately and to detect the reasons for any shortfalls'.

For security and other reasons, the palace also has a directly

employed cleaning force and comparisons between the two
computer analyses of the work provides a useful benchmark.
Even more important, the record can show longer-term trends to
identify emerging problems in a given area. For example,
difficulty in keeping a floor surface or drapes clean may indicate
that there is a need arising for refurbishment or replacement.

'The records also show the productivity levels we can stipulate
because records of improving trends may well go back for years,'
adds Good. 'That in turn gave us a more exact specification when
we were drawing up the invitation to tender. Beyond that, we
gave tenderers freedom to specify their materials, equipment and
methods and we judged them not only on efficiency but also on
environmental and conservation grounds.'

Many of the major cleaning contractors are themselves taking
the initiative to ensure efficient monitoring systems are in place.
As Geoff Tyler, author of an article on the subject, points out in
the July 31, 1997 issue of *Supply Management* magazine, many of
them are now adopting computer-based inspection methods.
Aramark, for example, uses a software system from FM
Workshop on hand-held computers. These computers are used
by Aramark inspectors as they and a manager from a client firm
do the rounds of two of the biggest food warehouses of two
major supermarket rivals in the UK.

'We plan our periodical quality audits,' says Des O'Neill, an
Aramark director, 'which use the data generated by these daily
cleaning inspections. But, more important, the software prompts
the users on the checks that need to be made and the results to be
recorded to ensure that nothing gets overlooked by accident. The
computer knows where it is by reading bar codes attached to key
items around the inspection route. At the end of the inspection,
the client representative electronically confirms their involvement and satisfaction with the result by keying a secret PIN code
into the computer.'

The company goes one further – the results are e-mailed to the
firm's head office so that each day's inspection can be reviewed

as soon as it has been completed. O'Neill insists that clients have come to expect cleaning contractors to use quality control methods as sophisticated as the ones they use in their own factories and offices.

Ken Smith, director of Workplace Management, also argues that the expectations from an outsourcing deal should be clearly set out in the service level agreement to avoid possible future misunderstandings. In an article on premises and facilities management outsourcing by Geoff Tyler in the 2 October, 1997 issue of *Supply Management* magazine, Smith observes: 'The key is to get the quality management right. During the compilation of the service level agreement both the client and outsourcing management contractor should study the detail of how the contractor will manage the individual services – cleaning, security, reception, maintenance and so on. They should also establish how the client will then manage the manager, and only the manager, to audit the outsourcing contract. The biggest single failure by clients is to continue to exercise the detailed management control they exercised before outsourcing was put in place – a duplication of effort.

'The client's role should be one of hands-off auditing at intervals established as optimum at the start of the contract. Also established should be the deliverables – what standards are required of the various services and how they will be measured. Without this discipline, the outsourcing project will be measured purely by anecdotal evidence of its mistakes, usually blown out of proportion.'

BBC Wales' headquarters in Cardiff has a premises and facilities management outsourcing contract with Select that is probably one of the most comprehensive ever set up in this area. It includes mainstream premises management functions such as catering, security, reception and staff, mailroom and staff, buildings maintenance, in-office printing, plus office and window cleaning. It also features services vital to the BBC's operations, such as IT and video-conferencing, mechanical engineering to maintain studio equipment and building plant, and studio bookings.

Jim Brown, head of resources at BBC Wales, advises that whether drawing up an initial or renewal tender, it is important to be precise about what services are to be provided and to what standard. For instance, in maintenance work, it is essential to specify both preventative maintenance routines and repair call-out times, perhaps categorizing plant and equipment according to urgency.

The monitoring mechanism is via Select's help-desk service. Says Brown: 'It is the central communication point for the facilities management operation. Help-desk staff have a facilities database and are responsible for all maintenance requests. Management reports are compiled each month for all services to assess trends and overall performance. We also have the right to vet any contractors' employees we deem unsuitable though we have seldom had to exercise it. Contractors' staff turnover is beyond our control, but taking care to show them they are accepted, as if they were BBC employees, has helped keep it to negligible levels.'

Over-control

Failure to monitor an outsource contract carefully can lead to serious consequences, but over-zealous control of the contractor can also cause unsatisfactory results. Duplication of effort will defeat the whole purpose of the exercise. It requires some finesse to outsource a complete business function with its staff and assets to a third-party and still retain a measure of control over the outcome. The danger is that the outsourcing company's management controls will remain in place, duplicating those of the contractor and placing an unnecessary brake on the freedom of the contractor to fulfil best-practice objectives. It can also leave the outsourced staff confused about who they really report to and who is measuring their performance. Such an illogical approach to outsourcing is both wasteful and unsustainable.

The link between the outsourcing organization and the contractor is often a single management appointee through whom all outsourced managerial decisions have to be filtered. In the worst scenario, the decisions that have to be approved via this channel can be as mundane as the deployment of personnel on shift work.

The management appointee may be a deliberate placement into a new post created expressly for the purpose. More often, he or she is the former manager of the in-house operation the outsourcing agreement is replacing and someone who probably should have been incorporated into that agreement or have been redeployed within the organization or made redundant.

The outsourcing contractor may end up with employees who are a mix of those transferred from the client company under Tupe (see Chapter 8) and staff the contractor has brought to the party. If an undue measure of management control is retained by the client organization these people will be working under confusing – and often conflicting – conditions. They should always be made aware that they are responsible to their employer – the contractor – and no one else when it comes to disciplinary issues. Complaints about behaviour relate to the fact that the contractor is not meeting the standards set out in the outsource agreement. These are issues that should be settled between the outsourcer and the contractor. Any decisions taken to arrive at a more satisfactory level of performance should be relayed to the outsourced staff by the contractor.

It is important to preserve relationships between staff involved in outsource contract and in-house services. In cleaning, for example, a case can be made out for treating premises management as a single outsourced entity because of the high level of employee deployment across boundaries embracing, for example, cleaning, building maintenance, grounds upkeep, building plant servicing and so on.

Equally, there are companies which see this as an 'eggs-in-one-basket' situation and argue that the liaison between individual contractors and in-house personnel is easy enough to establish. Regardless of the view taken, there will always be a boundary at which outsourced and in-house staff meet. The help desk staffed by an IT outsource contract for the express benefit of office computer users is another obvious example. 'Them and us' conflicts should be avoided at all costs by stipulating precisely in the outsource agreement how the operating relationships should work.

The danger of duplicated responsibilities by both contractor and client management is at its highest at such interfaces. Managers in general often have to work hard to develop delegation skills. In the same way, outsourcing organizations must learn to delegate to contractors with confidence. That confidence should stem from establishing in the outsourcing agreement the levels of service the contractor is expected to achieve and the recourse open to the client if the contractor falls short of these aims. Such issues should be at the heart of the service level agreement.

7
The Benefits and Pitfalls of Outsourcing

The PA Consulting Group's report, *Strategic Sourcing*, provides, for the first time, quantitative evidence of a positive correlation between high levels of outsourcing and share price performance. In PA's view, the findings demonstrate that efficient companies, which usually perform well in the market, are likely to see effective outsourcing as part of good management practice. However, as Malcolm Brown points out in an article on outsourcing in *Management Today*, the PA report also makes it very plain that the magic of outsourcing is not working for many – perhaps most – corporations. Only five per cent of more than 300 companies and public sector organizations investigated by the PA researchers found outsourcing high on benefits and low on drawbacks. For many of the rest, the outcome of such sub-contracting was either mediocre or a total flop.

Taken together, the two findings represent something of a conundrum for companies, suggests Brown. If you take the view that outsourcing really does improve the value of your organization, says PA's outsourcing expert John Little, 'then there's quite a lot to shoot for, but it's only worth shooting for if you're actually going to get it right. I rather tend to take the view that outsourcing is only worth doing well. If you aren't going to do it well, then don't do it at all. There are so many downsides to it.'

A similar conclusion was reached in a report by Deloitte & Touche, *Leading Trends in Information Services*, which found that a high proportion of users have been disappointed in outsourcing deals and are striving to improve performance on both sides. The survey of 1,400 chief information officers worldwide shows a high level of discontent. Findings include complaints that while 61 per cent had expected to benefit from a vendor's expertise, only 35 per cent actually achieved this; and while 52 per cent expected improved quality of IT, only 32 per cent received it.

'There was a significant shortfall in what officers expected from outsourcing and what they actually got,' says Martyn Thomas, global practice director at Deloitte & Touche.

Sharon Smith, writing in the *Daily Telegraph* supplement on outsourcing, attributes the dissatisfaction to a host of different factors, including users' lack of management over contracts and suppliers' failure to understand business needs. 'But most experts agree,' writes Smith, 'that the discontent is leading to companies shifting towards shorter, more flexible and partnership type contracts rather than following such bodies as the RAC, Virgin Direct and NEC, all of which have brought outsourced functions back in-house. For most organizations, large-scale retreats are deemed to be too costly and complicated.'

This more positive approach is supported by Andersen Consulting's report, *Vision 2010: Designing Tomorrow's Organization*, which says that companies expect outsourcing to continue to increase in importance, pointing towards the arrival of the virtual organization. Forty per cent of survey respondents predicted that their firms would be substantial or fully-fledged virtual corporations by 2010.

An Institute of Logistics survey of 300 companies that had outsourced their logistics to a third party or had pulled it back in-house revealed that many of them were largely dissatisfied with the service they had received. The main complaint, according to Denis O'Sullivan, who is a change management consultant for IBM, and who helped to conduct the survey, was that the providers were not being sufficiently proactive. 'The view was that the logistics service companies are doing what they are told by their clients, but it is the users who are coming up with the brightest ideas,' explains O'Sullivan.

Falling short of expectations

It was a question of falling short of expectations. The companies who were outsourcing their logistics regarded the service providers as the experts and the specialists and they were expected to be innovative as well as providing the service they had contracted to perform. The providers, in their turn, argue that it is not part of the deal for them to be innovative. Indeed, companies were still driving hard bargains and trying to get the service at the lowest possible cost and that left the service providers with such low profit margins that it was impossible to offer added-value in the form of innovation or anything else. A typical response from a director of a logistics firm provider is: 'I am not paid to be innovative. I am paid to get the basics right.'

The problem is that if both sides are counting on each other to be innovative and neither party sees it as its responsibility, the advances in new technology and new thinking are simply not going to happen. The logistics industry, in the UK at least, could end up being very static and is likely to fall behind in the race to win European-wide and international business.

Another mistake that companies made in the early days when handing over their logistics to a third-party service provider was to abdicate responsibility and lose all management control of the function. 'Anyone who says that distribution or logistics is not a core part of their business is effectively saying that the process of getting their products to the customer is not a core part of their business. That is totally wrong,' says O'Sullivan.

Although it happens less today, O'Sullivan has observed companies hand over their entire logistics department to a third-party, including the manager, and then delegate the monitoring of the service to a junior manager who may have little experience of the activity. 'That's a very expensive mistake. Most companies now realize that you really do have to retain the management of an outsourced operation, particularly where you've got something as complicated as a supply chain. Your concern as the outsourcer is not whether lorries are back on time, whether they've been maintained properly or whether there is enough space in the warehouse. What you are actually doing is managing a relationship and making sure the third-party service provider is reporting the right sort of information back to you. That's a different sort of skill. You could argue it requires greater skill than running the physical side of the business.'

Bob Aylott, of KPMG, stresses that it is vital to establish at the contract stage the kind of relationship that the outsourcing organization wants to forge with the provider. It is pointless, in his view, to expect a partnership type of relationship and then attempt to strike the tightest possible financial deal, unless it is agreed that other aspects of the relationship will be funded separately. Outsourcers are naïve if they expect to get something for nothing. The problem, suggests Aylott, is defining a contract that enshrines the outsourcer's expectations and has built into it the kind of reward structure that reflects aspects of the service that are not yet abundantly clear.

Framework for innovation
'The challenge today,' says Aylott, 'for most people who are defining outsourcing contracts – and this includes us – is to come up with a framework of a deal that actually encourages people to innovate, and rewards them and provides incentives to do that, as well as deliver a service. They're not inclusive, they're additive.'

KPMG runs workshops to help clients and their service providers decide the kind of relationship that works best for them and to establish realistic expectations from the chosen relationship. The categories of relationships vary from 'business supporter' – where the business value added is high to 'maintain IT service quality' – where the business value added is low – but where in both cases the risk-sharing is low. In the category of 'business partner' (high value added) and 'best in class IT service' (low value added), however, the risk-sharing is high.

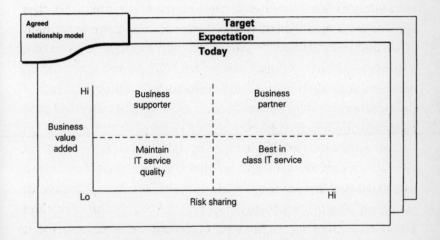

Source: KPMG Consultants

In Aylott's experience, outsourcers are less happy with the relationships they have forged with their providers than they were a few years ago, largely because their expectations have risen. 'Satisfaction is the relationship between perception and expectation. Expectations have risen. Perception of the service remains the same. Therefore the gap between perception and expectation has widened. *QED*: dissatisfaction. People are looking for ways in which they would be happier to work together. They want to get away from the transactional type relationship and move towards a partnering type of relationship. We help people in that area.'

KPMG has been running a study programme, as part of a broader project called *Impact*, which has been looking at the critical success factors that make relationship management more or less successful. The research has come up with fourteen critical success factors that KPMG judges to be important. It relates the critical success factors to the desired benefits of the outsourcing project. Some benefits and some relationships emerge as more dependent on some critical success factors than others. This gives outsourcing clients an opportunity to focus on the critical success factors relevant to the benefits and relationships they are seeking. It also helps to arrive at a gap analysis between perception and expectation. In a workshop situation the outsourcing organization and the provider may discover that they have totally different perceptions of how well or not a service is being provided. While one provider may think it is doing well on certain critical success factors, the outsourcer may have an entirely different view. Such discrepancies are exposed as a result of the data collection involved in the exercise.

Too often outsourcers wait until their relationship with their provider is close to the divorce stage before they think about undertaking this kind of partnership therapy. Aylott compares it to marital conflict. 'People only go to a lawyer when they decide a divorce is imminent. KPMG doesn't have a Relate type service. We have very much a divorce type service.'

Recognizing this gap in the market, Aylott has set up an independent company called the Outsourcing Management Group which is concerned with the ongoing management of outsourcing and making that successful. It is a support-focused organization as opposed to the project-focused service provided by KPMG.

Venturing into the unknown

In the initial stages of its IT outsourcing project, BP Exploration encountered the kind of setbacks that are commonly experienced by outsourcers venturing into the unknown. According to John Cross, head of IT for the BP Group, the first few months of the implementation were particularly rocky.

'While senior managers at BP and at the three suppliers clearly understood the vision of seamless service captured in the framework agreements, their respective operations staffs did not. One supplier's employees looked to us to set directions for them, as they would in any traditional outsourcing contract. They wanted to follow orders, whereas we insisted that they look for ways to make the operations run more efficiently and effectively. Another supplier staffed a site primarily with former BP employees (who under the agreement became employees of the supplier) and very few of its own managers. As a result, the services we had long supplied to ourselves continued as if nothing had changed; the supplier did not bring in any new ideas or improve the operations. Eventually, the suppliers replaced middle management on the sites and the situation improved quickly.'

BP itself shoulders some of the blame for these early setbacks. 'We mistakenly set cost reduction as the most important target for our suppliers to achieve during the first year,' explains Cross. 'The provider who added too few of its own staff to our former IT site, for example, was working under particularly stringent cost targets. In 1994, we shifted the emphasis from costs to service responsiveness, quality, and customer satisfaction.'

Even when the project was fairly well established, BP Exploration did not find itself entirely free from the task of managing conflicts among its suppliers. Observed Cross in an article he wrote for the May/June 1995 issue of the *Harvard Business Review*: 'They worked well together to deliver day-to-day service to us, in part because they are so independent. But they are also rivals competing for our future business. As a result, they are reluctant to share, for instance, best practice with one another. If a company responsible for one site, say, solves a common problem with the interconnections between different personal computers, or develops a help service that BP managers at the site like, the company is reluctant to share this information with its two competitors. Why? Because the knowledge or service may become part of the supplier's pitch for additional business during future contract negotiations.'

Nevertheless, Cross was able to report some considerable gains from the IT outsourcing project: 'Our IT costs continue to fall. Through consolidation and outsourcing, we reduced our IT staff by 80 per cent and our overall operating costs have fallen from $360 million in 1989 to $132 million in 1994. We have increased the proportion of IT costs that are variable and adjustable to business conditions. We have gained greater flexibility in our systems and higher quality IT services. And it has become increasingly apparent that service companies provide us with technical skills and ideas that we could no longer develop inside our own company. For instance, we are exploring ways to use virtual-reality technologies, such as desk-top teleconferencing and other multimedia applications that facilitate virtual meetings, to enhance organizational effectiveness inside BP.'

Five years on, BP decided to integrate its IT activities across all its main business streams and set about outsourcing the greater part of it, based on the lessons learned from the BP Exploration experience. Cross was still convinced that an alliance of contractors was the right way to go, but an important lesson for him was to avoid using contractors from common service lines in a common alliance. He admits that with the original BP Exploration IT contract he felt it was the right thing to do 'because, to be honest, at that point we were very much less sure of the competency of an organization and, I guess, even our own judgement to pick an organization that would be sustainably successful. Our happy notion was that it was like a double-barrelled shotgun – if one failed you always had a second shot because there was always a back-up service provider who already knew your operation – and that it would be very easy for that second supplier to move across and pick up the pieces.'

However, the downside was that whenever BP Exploration had two suppliers managing the same service across different areas, they were not prepared to share their experiences. 'As we began to integrate our sites more and more and create a more networked corporation we found the inter-dependence of different sites became much higher and the need for service interchange became higher,' recalls Cross. 'You began to find that the different companies didn't behave very well across those boundaries in terms of sharing what they were doing or working in co-operation with each other. It led to an unreasonable amount of antipathy and that, in the end, of course, affects the service. You often found you were having to adjudicate.'

In addition, Cross found to his consternation that the suppliers 'would regard the service knowledge they acquired on site as part of their competitive product offering. The last thing they really wanted to do was share that experience, which was actually learned at BP expense, with their fellow "competitor".'

Learning from that lesson, BP has subsequently determined to make certain that only one player represents each of the service lines. 'Again, we have not gone for a model that says any one player will do everything well,' stresses Cross. 'We are still not confident about that, but we have found that provided they are in different business segments, like telecommunications, for example, most of them don't have any aspirations for other parts of the business, so they should work well together.'

Applying these lessons to the whole of BP's IT sector, however, throws up problems. Like many multinationals, BP has organizations spread around the globe that have each gone their separate ways in deciding the extent to which outsourcing is appropriate. 'When I look across the total global stage it's a real curate's egg with bits of normal operation going on, particularly in places like the Far East where outsourcing has been very late into the game,' says Cross. 'The whole cultural environment there is of self-exclusivity on anything you are doing. They just, by and large, don't like the notion that you ever do anything outside your organization. As a result, the service industry has been slow to develop in the Asia Pacific region.'

Nevertheless, by early 1998 plans were well in hand to outsource most of the IT functions that were currently being done in-house at BP. Cross predicts that eventually the 1,000 IT staff throughout BP will be reduced to 'around 200 top flight professionals who work in-house and in essence manage the service lines from the outside market'.

At the time of writing this book, BP had shortlisted four major IT service providers, one of which was destined to be the lead partner in a new alliance. The plan was that the winner would take over the entire global service line connected with the desk-top PC operations and the global networks, plus all the support and maintenance involved. 'BP has moved into a very network-centric model of computing anyway, so the servers and the PCs on the desks and all the wires that bind them together pretty much define the scope of the area, as well as the help desk behind that,' elaborates Cross. 'Whoever wins that contest has to work in conjunction with the other major supplier which is BT for the telecommunications side of the business. We also have differing outsourcing agreements with those who support and sustain our applications portfolio. Because there are significant differences in the functional skills around applications, there are different suppliers handling that and they are very focused on that part of the service. There is no overlap, so there is no back-biting across the various organizations. That's what we've really tried to remove this time around. The big lesson for us has been to be very much more clearly defined and ring-fenced around the areas of service delivery.'

Grappling with innovation
One issue that BP is still grappling with, however, is how to generate a greater level of innovation amongst its service

providers. 'The technology innovation side was probably the greatest failure of all,' admits Cross. 'None of the service providers really were all that good and we have thought and worried about that long and hard. It's something that bothers us still. As a result I have created and held on to a much more powerful internal technology strategy group as a core competency because I haven't been able to trust the market's ability to deliver that for me. There's no reason why they shouldn't be able to provide that, yet the irony is they don't. I have a feeling that BP is as much to blame for that. I am not sure whether we have created enough of a climate of opportunity to give them scope to discover and work on that.'

BP has, however, found a way to measure and reward quality of service. Suppliers can improve on their profit margins by up to four per cent based on independent customer–client surveys of the perception of service. A bad score can mean that one per cent is lopped off a service provider's profit margin. Cross introduced the scheme after he found that there was too much emphasis on cost-saving at the expense of quality. 'You have to design the incentive scheme around the key issues you want attention paid to,' he points out. 'The things that get measured and rewarded are the things that get focused on. It's a very simple axiom of life.'

To sustain the focus on the important issues, BP has downgraded measurement of what Cross calls 'engine room data.' He says, 'In a sense, that's the supplier's responsibility. But in the beginning we thought we had to measure physical uptime of hardware and service and everything else.'

In fact, Cross discovered that the service providers could claim a 97 per cent score for operational efficiency, but the users would still complain that it was lousy. 'Operational statistics like that do not necessarily tie in to perceptions of what happened to the end user,' he observes. 'The three per cent default happened at a very critical part of a month where the businesses absolutely needed full availability and it all happened in one chunk. Ninety-seven per cent over the month really isn't a very satisfactory way of viewing that. We have learned that there is a need to be much more focused on what the business perception of those things are, rather than what all the internal engine room statistics are.'

BP will inevitably continue to fine tune its approach to IT outsourcing, but none of the ups and downs of past experience have shaken Cross's faith in the technique as the right way for BP to go. 'The issue around why we outsource has remained as relevant today as it has always been. More importantly, I have a good track record which sustains my belief that it was an absolutely essential thing to have done. It's about focus of the organization. Running large operational centres, whether they are building systems or running on physical computers, is actually a very managerially time-demanding activity, especially in a large organization. It is managerially demanding not just because the focus of the operational agenda is always critical to a business, but it is actually just physically looking after people. If you have a thousand staff to worry about that is a managerially-demanding activity, whether you like it or not.'

Other parts of BP, however, have been more sceptical about the value of IT outsourcing and it has required a degree of persuasion in some quarters. It usually boils down to the perception of senior management running the IT operations of a particular business sector. A new man took over at BP's chemicals division and immediately saw outsourcing as the way to go. Others have perhaps been more inclined to hang on to the team they have built up over a considerable number of years and which they are reluctant to see disbanded or transferred to an entirely different organization with perhaps a less conducive culture.

Cross, however, has no regrets about seeing the BP Exploration in-house IT workforce reduced from 1,400 to a mere 100 professionals completely focused on 'the value generation of technology appliance', as he puts it. In his view, it all boils down to what senior management of an IT operation should worry about. 'My argument has always been that we should be worrying about our business and how to improve its performance in the context of smart technology application. The real beauty of outsourcing for me is that it really only leaves me with two things to do – one is worry with my senior business executives about what they are trying to do in terms of their business agenda and the second is worry about what's going on in the market place, which is growing at a stupendous rate. Then I guess my value lies in my capability, which is combining my mix of business understanding and where the focus of future challenges lie and coupling that with where new technologies may be able to make substantial improvements. That's what I would call the value opportunity agenda as distinct from the service operational agenda, which is an engine room one.'

Best practice
Research conducted by the Centre for Business Strategy and Procurement at Birmingham Business School suggests that only about 20 per cent of organizations have what it would consider to be 'a best practice outsourcing decision-making methodology'. This comes as no surprise to Dr Chris Lonsdale, a member of the centre. 'Most other firms are either using a methodology that is static in its focus, i.e. it focuses on what is core at the present time, or they do not have a strategy and are chasing cost and headcount-reducing opportunities in an *ad hoc* manner. It is not surprising, therefore, that many organizations report that they are experiencing problems with outsourcing.'

Lonsdale declares that it is time for organizations to ignore the hype and reject the conventional wisdom about outsourcing, and instead develop 'make-buy methodologies that are tailored to their own specific circumstances. Only then will they achieve the improvements they seek in terms of cost, quality and delivery.'

Positive evidence
There is plenty of evidence to suggest that if outsourcing is carefully planned and a proper process put in place for evaluating

providers and for monitoring their future performance, there are real benefits to be enjoyed.

BOC's use of the SESPA process to evaluate outsource providers has undoubtedly reaped dividends. When Craig Lardner trawls through the thirty-four attributes that BOC Australia drew up before inviting bids for the outsourcing of its legal services, he can point to numerous advantages from putting the service into the hands of a single external firm of lawyers. Referring to the responsiveness attribute, for example, he points out that now, when a BOC line manager comes up with a legal issue that needs to be addressed, the response time is much faster than it used to be when it involved a multitude of suppliers. 'There's an improved level of service provision as viewed by the user of the service – the line manager who needs the legal advice,' claims Lardner.

The important point, adds Lardner, is that the evaluation process involves a measure by which to gauge the satisfaction of the end-user. 'Without surveying internal users in the first place you are left to your own best guess which is hardly well-founded.'

Another benefit is that Middletons Moore & Bevins (MMB), the Australian law firm that won the outsourcing bid, has a prescribed problem-solving model. It is a TQM (Total Quality Management) technique, which both BOC and the outsource provider are familiar with. 'When we have a problem to sort out, we are using the same process,' says Lardner. 'We don't talk a different language to each other.'

BOC's SESPA model for the legal outsourcing also covers conflicts of interest. 'We have a process in place that flags up any conflicts of interest. Our legal advisers were required to show us what they do when we put a legal matter to them, to make sure they don't have any conflicts of interest with another party we are involved with,' elaborates Lardner. 'There's a minimum risk in this area because a process is in place. Before, when it was with twenty-four different law firm suppliers, it may have been brought to our attention, maybe not. One of the bidders for the outsourcing had to disqualify themselves because when they searched their records they found they were acting on behalf of one of BOC's direct competitors on a matter. The scary thing is, that firm had advised us before on some matters, but because they are such a big firm they didn't know about it.'

One of the biggest gains from the outsourcing was reduced costs involved in retaining one legal firm rather than the previous twenty-four practices. 'That means that the volume of work this one legal firm is getting from BOC justifies it dealing with us wholeheartedly rather than just superficially,' points out Lardner. 'They are getting the whole of our business rather than one-24th of it. It would be unreasonable of us as a customer to expect them to go out of their way to understand BOC and the industrial gases business and represent us fully if we are only giving them one-24th of our business. If you give them all the business, as long as single-sourcing doesn't represent a risk in itself, they can afford to spend the time to get to know BOC well.'

Yet another benefit to come from the outsourcing partnership with the legal firm is computer compatibility – something BOC could not have expected when it was dealing with over twenty separate practices. The result is excellent communications.

Single point of contact

What BOC classifies as 'familiarity and continuity of staff' is another gain. Instead of having to deal with twenty-four contacts at the individual law firms, BOC now has one point of contact at the legal firm who channels all the dealings in both directions. It could be imagined that the snag to all this was the fact that BOC now has all its eggs in one basket – that no single law firm could be expected to have high levels of expertise in all the different aspects of legal advice that a major corporation like BOC is likely to encounter in its lifetime.

Lardner believes BOC has this danger covered. Part of the evaluation process involved scoring the law firm on thirteen different skills or areas of legal expertise, such as financial, IT, technical, property, employee relations, environmental law, joint ventures, dispute resolution and tax advice. It would be unreasonable to have expected a single law firm to be pre-eminent in these skills in every part of Australia. When BOC launched the bidding process it was not at all convinced it would find one solitary law firm that could claim to have all these areas covered right across the board. It was quite open to the idea that it might have to outsource to two or three law firms in order to cover the full range of expertise. That, of course, would have been a great improvement on the twenty-four firms BOC Australia was already using.

However, the company that won the business was able to show that if it was not represented in a particular part of the country on property issues, for example, it would appoint affiliates it could vouch for to cover the gap.

The single sourcing has the added advantage that BOC Australia, which used to get bills from twenty-four separate law firms a month, now gets only one bill from one law firm. BOC further asked the bidders for the legal service how they could contribute to reducing the industrial gases company's costs over time. A number of them, including MMB, came up with ideas that demonstrated how they could provide the same service year-on-year at a reduced overall cost level.

Access to leading-edge technology was another attribute that BOC Australia sought in its supplier of legal services. The contenders for the outsourcing contract were asked what they could offer on this score. MMB, the successful bidder, offered a CD-ROM that contained all the changes in the law that had happened in the previous month, cutting down enormously on the amount of paperwork needed to be scanned by BOC's in-house lawyers. The law firm even offered to highlight the law changes that were most relevant to BOC and its field of operations. In addition, MMB agreed to a request from BOC Australia that allows the gases company's in-house lawyers to use the law firm's library facilities.

The outsourcing deal with MMB has developed with these kinds of initiatives into a partnership that is mutually beneficial to both parties. For example, a legal graduate from MMB now spends one day a week at BOC Australia helping with legal issues. Both sides gain. 'The graduate learns about industry from the inside. MMB gets an experienced individual faster than would normally have been the case because he or she is operating in the real corporate world. What we get is the resource,' says Lardner. 'We had to commit, not unreasonably, that this person would not spend the time doing filing or photocopying. It had to be substantial work that would be of benefit to a graduate.'

The experiment has been so successful that graduates at MMB have been queuing up to take part in the scheme, following the enthusiastic reaction of the first assignee.

Mirror image

Lardner emphasizes that for an outsourcing deal to work it is just as important for the customer to adopt the right attitude as it is for the supplier to meet the customer's needs. 'If we are going to ask some extremely rigorous things of our suppliers we should stand in the mirror and impose the same standards on ourselves. We as the customer have to go through a bit of a metamorphosis too. We have to get the competency matrix up on the table. We have to be prepared to talk about it and why something is important to us that may not be important to somebody else. We want to achieve best customer status. When we are not around we want the supplier to say, "BOC is our best customer", not based on how much we buy, but on many other criteria.'

Striving to achieve best customer status calls for a substantial change of mind-set, in Lardner's view:

Customer of yesterday	Best customer status
Pays when pushed and by cheque	Pays as promised and electronically
Will give you a hearing when you have something new	Expects you to develop the new, gives you ideas on what might be new and helps you to develop the new
Calls the supplier a vendor	Calls the supplier a supplier
Will set up an agreement to buy that must be re-negotiated sooner rather than later	Never wants to re-negotiate ever again. Invests that time in developing the relationship
Selfish	Unselfish/innovative
Win/lose	Win/win
Mine/yours	Ours

THE ADVANTAGES OF OUTSOURCING TO A THIRD-PARTY PROVIDER

• A firm that specialises in outsourcing can usually bring better qualified people to address both day-to-day and strategic issues facing companies than they are likely to employ on their own. And the company only pays for the services and time it needs.

• Outsourced staff are given the opportunity to be focused. They are concerned about their performance – their whole reputation and future employment is based on it and consequently they have a vested interest in performing well. It is human nature for full-time staff to be more complacent about their stability, but to outsourced staff, deadlines, reputations and jobs go hand in hand.

• Third-parties, who are focusing on serving several customers, can realize economies of scale that a single company could not possibly achieve. They can spread the cost of research, purchasing, training, marketing and consulting over many customers. Third-party staff who have been trained and are up-to-date on new technologies are less likely to make costly on-the-job decisions than those who do not completely understand the technology and alternatives. Also, third-parties can afford a higher quality and wider assortment of tools than a single company can expect to do.

• Markets, competition, government regulations, financial conditions and technology all change extremely quickly. When companies outsource they become more flexible, more dynamic and better able to change to meet these variable opportunities. Outsourcing providers make investments that take the risks across a broad spectrum of companies, effectively allowing an individual company to become far more responsive to these changes, indeed to thrive on them.

• Third-party staff can often provide knowledge and experience in the various options that technology allows, and in the identification and resolution of problems that may crop up with the technology.

• Using third-party staff may be more cost-effective and a quicker way of increasing skill levels than hiring new staff. Outsourcing can help focus on the functions that add the most business value. You can outsource the non-strategic activators and spend more time on important and profitable work.

• By the very nature of their specialization, outsourcing providers can bring extensive worldwide, world-class capabilities to meeting the needs of their customers.

THE DISADVANTAGES OF OUTSOURCING TO A THIRD-PARTY PROVIDER

• Employees who have worked for some time in an organization have accumulated knowledge and understanding that will take time for the staff of a third-party contractor to acquire. This problem will be less acute when the staff of the outsourcing organization are transferred to the provider as part of the deal.

• Every company is different with its own culture and methods of operation. It will inevitably take time for these characteristics to be assimilated by a third-party provider. It may be, of course, that the contractor will want to change some of these methodologies to achieve economies of scale and greater efficiency, in which case there will be a difficult transition period while everyone makes the necessary adjustment.

• In the event of the staff of the outsourcing company being transferred to the third-party provider, there will be those who adapt more readily to the new culture than others. It will take time to discover who has transferred smoothly and who is experiencing difficulty adapting to the new climate.

• If a partnership arrangement is sought with the third-party provider, it will inevitably undergo teething troubles in the early stages. There are likely to be misunderstandings about what exactly is expected from the outsourcing deal. Reality will in all probability fall short of expectations and there will need to be constant reviews to pinpoint where the partnership is not working.

• In a partnership arrangement there will need to be a high degree of trust and openness. However, it will be hard for the outsourcing company to reveal confidential information it is used to guarding closely, and indeed there may be delicate information it may regard it prudent not to make known to outsiders. If the outsourcer is too coy about the information it is reluctant to reveal it may put pressure on the partnership relationship.

• If a company is outsourcing a particular activity to more than one contractor, it may find it difficult to manage the relationships between all the parties concerned. Even if the multiple providers have agreed to co-operate with each other at the outset, expect some border disputes at various stages and do not be surprised if one provider tries to poach from another's agreed domain.

• Dependence on a single provider for a particular outsourced function will reduce the number of relationships that need to be managed, but the outsourcer needs to be careful that the single provider has expertise across the board, or at least has access to expertise in areas of weakness. Security of information is likely to be less under threat, however, with a one-to-one relationship.

THE FUTURE

Outsourcers and providers will continue to explore ways of working together to achieve seamless co-operation. As confidence grows organizations can be expected to outsource an increasing number of operations that were previously regarded as sacrosanct and best kept in-house. Whether or not the so-called virtual organization ever becomes a widespread phenomenon is explored in Chapter 9. In the meantime, there will be new challenges that will test the efficacy of outsourcing and the patience of those trying to make it work.

The two most immediate challenges are likely to be dealing with the advent of the Euro currency and the much-discussed threat of the millennium time-bomb. The latter, if not handled with care, could cause untold chaos to computer systems around the world. The problem is that most computers are programmed to recognize two-digit dates (i.e. 98 rather than 1998). Unless the systems are re-programmed, computers will simply recognize the year 2000 as two zeros, which could bring businesses, airlines and a host of other computer-controlled systems to a grinding halt. The nightmare scenario could include whole plants breaking down, security locks jamming and heating systems and air conditioning refusing to work. The idea of computers on board aircraft going berserk on the eve of the millennium doesn't bear thinking about.

The cost of ensuring that none of these potential disasters actually happen is astronomical for companies and organizations around the world. ICI, for example, is reported to be spending £80 million on the year 2000 problem and a further £10 million dealing with the arrival of the Euro.

With major companies spending this kind of money on dealing with the problems their end, they are expecting suppliers and outsource providers to do their bit to make sure they don't put a spanner in the works. ICI, for example, has warned thousands of its suppliers that they will lose key contracts if they fail to take timely measures to start dealing in the Euro and to resolve the millennium bug issue. The company has made it clear that businesses will be at a competitive disadvantage if they have not made the necessary currency changes and dealt with the year 2000 problem which could bring production to a halt overnight if computers crash. ICI contracts with companies throughout Europe, worth £7 billion annually, are at risk.

Clearly, with the trend towards single-source suppliers, it will be those companies that are quick off the mark in dealing with these critical threats to the smooth-running of the supplier-partnership that will emerge as the winners in the twenty-first century.

8
Who Am I Working For?

Apart from being sacked, there can be few more disconcerting experiences for an individual than being outsourced. The daunting prospect of being transferred to a different organization in a different location with perhaps an entirely different corporate culture will inevitably fill most people with foreboding in the first instance. However, once the initial shock has been absorbed, many will realize that the benefits of being outsourced can – and often do – outweigh the disadvantages. IT specialists, for example, may well ultimately relish the idea of moving from a department where they are by and large peripheral to the main business to an organization where they are surrounded and understood by fellow IT professionals. 'You are the business, not a support activity,' suggests Bob Aylott of KPMG.

It is a view echoed by Edmond Cunningham, principal consultant with PA Consulting and chairman of the outsourcing special interest group in the Computing Services and Software Association: 'People are going to an organization whose core business is what they do. They can expand and build their career.'

The outsourced individuals also can take heart in the knowledge that their terms of employment will be protected in the transfer under the terms of the Transfer of Undertakings (Protection of Employment) Regulations, a 1981 European Union directive, more familiarly known as Tupe. The directive is designed to guarantee that outsourced staff get a new job with the new company on the same terms and conditions as they had before. 'The essence of Tupe is that employees won't lose out,' says Cunningham.

According to Tim Ring, writing in the *Daily Telegraph* outsourcing supplement, Tupe's protection goes quite deep. 'No one involved in the transfer can be sacked except for some very narrow economic, technical or organizational reasons. Even if the outsourcing company gets its new employees to accept worse terms and conditions, such an agreement is not legal. And trade union recognition stays in force as long as the transferred unit remains an identifiably separate unit.'

The flexibility the individual may enjoy is not handicapped by such regulations, however. As Geoff Tyler, writing in *Supply Management* magazine, points out, in essence Tupe regulations require the contractor to become responsible for the employment or redundancy of the employees formerly engaged in the contracted activities. 'That does not mean, however, that they have to remain so engaged for ever. Once in the employ of the contractor they may transfer to work for a different client, accept promotion to the contractor's own office and so on as normal in their new careers. The extent to which they can be forced to move to a new project will depend on what is considered reasonable in the circumstances surrounding the matter and on the extent to which any revised conditions of employment to which they agreed are considered applicable.'

This sounds as though everything is loaded in favour of the transferred employees, but the same employment conditions do not translate into the same corporate climate or culture. As Ring suggests, employees could be moving from a cosy backwater to a hard-nosed commercial environment. Will they cut it? Will they fit in? Will they have to keep moving locations?

Observes Aylott: 'For some people that's a challenge. For other people it is an awful awesome responsibility that they've never had to handle before. Often when people transfer they look at Tupe and they think it is going to be the same over there as where they are coming from. They mistakenly think having the same contract is the same culture.'

An individual's terms of contract may, for example, entitle him or her to a company car, but when they move to the new organization they may find the model of car they are allowed to use is a lot more restricted than was the case with their previous company. There are other people for whom the job they are doing is a vocation. It is the organization they work for that is important to them. The kind of job they do is incidental. When they are transferred all that changes.

Aylott gives an example: 'There are people I know who were in the Health Service and they said: "I'm in IT, but I joined the Health Service because I actually wanted to join the Health Service, not because I was in the IT department. The Health Service was where my skills could best be applied." They feel very disenfranchised by being forced to join the supplier. They would have happily been a porter, let's say, instead of a programmer, if it meant they could stay in the Health Service. Generally speaking, that is not the case, but I know for a fact there are people in that category. Equally, there are people who felt that being second line was less threatening, less demanding. They were more comfortable in that position.'

In Aylott's experience, however, the majority of people transferred under an outsourcing agreement end up considering it to have been a good move. 'If you are ambitious it widens the markets for your skills within an organization. It also means the value of your skills is more sharply recognized in terms of their commercial exploitation basically, and their ability to leverage other people's skills.'

Handling the transition

Much of the responsibility for ensuring the smooth transfer of outsourced staff falls upon the shoulders of the service providers. For them this burgeoning market represents big business. One of Europe's largest IT service providers is Cap Gemini. The UK arm, which was formerly known as Hoskyns before it was taken over by French-based Cap Gemini Sogeti in 1990, had a turnover of around £40 million in 1997, 55 per cent of which came from outsourcing. A growing part of its outsourcing operations is what it calls business process management. When, for example, anyone books a seat at a local Virgin cinema via a Freefone number, the transaction is handled by Cap Gemini staff based in the North of Scotland. Similarly, Cap Gemini handles back office parking ticket processing for some of the London boroughs.

At the other end of the scale, Cap Gemini has been involved in some of the largest outsourcing deals known to the UK, including a ten-year contract involving 629 IT personnel in British Gas and over 600 IT people transferred from British Steel.

When it is decided to transfer employees from the outsourcer to the service provider, there are a number of key concerns that make it imperative the transaction is handled with the utmost care and delicacy. The IT director of the client firm will be concerned that the members of the team he has built up over a number of years are going to be looked after properly and absorbed into the service provider without too much disruption to any of their lives, and that their career prospects will be sustained, if not enhanced. The entire senior management of the outsourcing company will be anxious that the transition takes place with the minimum of disruption to the efficient running of the organization, as will, of course the service provider. The worst scenario for both outsourcer and service provider is that the IT team decides to resign en bloc.

'That's a worry we have on our side,' says Mike Dodsworth, human resources manager at Cap Gemini UK, 'because on day one, when we take responsibility for that service, you have to have people who know that system. Whilst it's a fact of life that if there are let's say fifty people in an IT department, Cap Gemini could probably replace all of them overnight in terms of technical competence, what we cannot provide on day one is the knowledge of the system.

'So we have two priorities around the transfer. The first is to keep the business going as usual – and improve it if we can – while at the same time paying attention to the personal aspirations of the staff involved in the transfer. My role is, firstly in a sales support mode, to convince the potential client's HR and IT staff that Cap Gemini knows how to look after people. They're not just human resources in the blandest sense of that word; they're people and the client is anxious that we will look after them.'

Benefit of the doubt
The process starts with a presentation to the IT team members about to be outsourced to convince them that they will be no worse off under the transfer from a financial point of view. Cap Gemini asks the IT people at the presentation to give it the benefit of the doubt. 'We say: give us a chance. Whatever your prejudices about Cap Gemini or organizations of our kind, work with us for a while.'

Reactions to such appeals inevitably vary. Some feel reassured. Others can react in a less positive way. Dodsworth cites the example of a colleague who was transferred from a leading white goods manufacturer to Cap Gemini in 1987. In those days there was no requirement for prior consultation with employees. Dodsworth's colleague was simply summoned to his boss's office one morning and informed that as of midnight he and the rest of the IT team had become employees of Hoskyns (now Cap Gemini). The man listened as a representative from Hoskyns told him what was going to happen under the terms of the transfer. His reaction was: 'This is all well and good, but if I had wanted to work for Hoskyns I would have applied to that organization in the first place. I don't like being forced to go and work for other people. I like making my own decisions, so I'll go and find a job'. He didn't resign, but he contacted some employment agencies and after about three months he received his first job offer.

On the train home after the job interview, he started to ponder about his position. He thought to himself: 'Do I really want to accept this job I've just been offered? What do I really know about this company? I've had an hour's interview. I was allowed ten minutes to ask questions and they showed me around the office. It seemed all right, but I've been working with this Hoskyns lot for three months now and they seem to have honoured every undertaking they've given. Maybe I should give it another three months and see how I get on.' That was 1987 and the man is now firmly ensconced in Cap Gemini.

Sometimes the residue of an IT department that was outsourced to Cap Gemini under a previous deal, is finally transferred. Cap Gemini then takes the opportunity to invite to a presentation the staff that have already been transferred for some time to chat with the people who are about to be transferred. At one such presentation to a group of IT people from an insurance company who were about to be transferred to Cap Gemini under an outsourcing deal, a previous employee mingled with those yet to go through the experience to tell them it was the best thing that had ever happened to her.

Having worked in the insurance company for years, this IT specialist had been looking for broader horizons, but was told by an employment agency she would have difficulty with her qualifications finding a higher level job in another company. When the outsourcing opportunity came along, she jumped at it because it provided the very chance she was seeking to move into a broader band of career options. She was happy to tell the uncertain IT people who had yet to be transferred all the new experiences she had enjoyed since joining Cap Gemini, which would never have happened within the in-house environment of an insurance company.

Dodsworth recognizes, however, that in any group of transferees there will be people who have a greater affinity with the nature of the organization they originally worked for than with their specialized skills in IT, for example. This was a particular issue when Cap Gemini undertook the outsourcing contract for the residuary body set up to wind down the former Greater London Council. Over 300 people joined Cap Gemini under that deal and around 100 are still working for it today. 'A lot of the people left reasonably quickly afterwards because their consciences could not cope with the idea of working for a profit-making organization as opposed to one providing a public service,' explains Dodsworth. 'Much as I tried to convince them that they were still giving that public service, albeit through another organization, they weren't happy with the idea. They felt the need to leave and return to the public sector – and it was very noticeable that that is where they all went.'

In the case of the IT people from the insurance company, Cap Gemini was able to reassure them that they could continue in the same line of business if they so wished as Cap Gemini has an insurance division of its own. On the other hand, they could broaden their experience if they preferred to venture into new fields.

Transitional team

Initially, Cap Gemini provides a transitional team to work alongside the staff about to be outsourced, hoping to make the transfer as smooth as possible. 'Whilst the initial suspicion is that the transition team is there to suck all the knowledge out of them so that they become surplus to requirements and we get rid of them, nothing could be further from the truth,' insists Dodsworth, 'because when you're recruiting in the large numbers that Cap Gemini is (around 2,000 a year) every IT person is valuable to us and we certainly don't want to discard any of them.'

Cap Gemini tries to allay any fears the transferring people have by sitting down with them on a one-to-one basis to discuss their future aspirations. 'That's when we measure "the best thing that ever happened to me", "the worst thing that ever happened to me",' elaborates Dodsworth. 'For most people of course, it is somewhere in the middle. We have to deal with their expectations, because some of them will think they've now got this instant opportunity to start a new career, some will be scared stiff that we will force them to do things they don't want to do and others will be in a wait-and-see mode.'

The transferring staff are individually asked whether, in an ideal world, they would like an alternative role in Cap Gemini at the earliest opportunity. Some will be enthusiastic about the idea. Others are likely to prefer to stay with the familiar workload for as long as possible. Others will want to bide their time and see what comes their way. 'We need to know their aspirations so that we can plan for the individual,' says Dodsworth. 'If there is someone who is very keen to move within Cap Gemini, we are going to lose them unless we can meet that aspiration. But we have the constraint of continuing the service to the client.'

In such cases, Cap Gemini will bring in someone from its organization to share the knowledge of the new transferee. Once the shadow operator is up to speed and can take over, the newcomer is released to pursue career opportunities in other parts of the Cap Gemini empire. The client company is sometimes nervous about taking this route, especially if it is a key member of the IT team. The client sometimes takes some convincing that this is in the best interests of all parties. 'My view is once individuals go and work for somebody entirely different, we've lost them – both the client and Cap Gemini are the losers. If, on the other hand, I move that individual from that workload to another part of the Cap Gemini empire, at the end of the day, if something really disastrous happens we at least know he or she is at the end of the phone line. They can even be brought back for a day to help sort it out, because they're still an employee of ours. In any case, constraining people against their wishes makes no sense. The whole drift of Cap Gemini's HR approach is that we are offering new opportunities. We are sensitive to people's requirements.'

End of the line?

One question that often occurs to people is that outsourcing contracts are often for five years. What happens when that time runs out? Dodsworth believes Cap Gemini has an enviable record when this eventuality occurs: 'We hope of course that the five years will become another five years, but they may not. The outsourcing company may have had a specific goal for the service of finite duration. Contracts can change hands. We may lose the contract to one of our competitors and under Tupe the people can go with it. We pride ourselves that when this situation has arisen we don't lose very many people to our competitors. They tend to stay with us.

'The best way to do it of course is to make them contract independent. They may join Cap Gemini as a member of an insurance company's IT team, or whatever, but after a year they may become a Cap Gemini employee and when a particular contract comes to an end they simply return to the pool of resource to be employed elsewhere. So you shake people out of their old ways slowly and sympathetically.'

An interesting observation Dodsworth has made is that the more hostile an individual is to the idea of being outsourced, the more likely he or she is to become a successful and long-standing Cap Gemini employee. He cites the example of one man who had worked for his organization for thirty-two years and was extremely hostile to the idea of being uprooted under an outsourcing deal. He exploded at the counselling session and demanded a redundancy payment. He later changed his mind, however, and now, still with Cap Gemini, admits his initial reaction was totally unfounded.

Avoiding an administrative nightmare
Tupe regulations could represent an administrative nightmare for an organization like Cap Gemini, which takes over huge workforces under some of its more high profile outsourcing deals. For example, in March 1998, over 600 IT staff were transferred to Cap Gemini under an outsourcing deal with British Steel. Providing each transferring employee with precisely the same terms and conditions of employment that they previously enjoyed, as Tupe stipulates, makes tremendous demands on the service provider, but Robert Ingram, Cap Gemini UK's HR director, overcomes this problem by offering transferring staff what he considers to be better conditions than the Tupe minimum.

'What we try to do,' he says, 'is behave in a reasonable way. Our principles are that we minimize the disruption to individuals as much as possible on transfer and then give them an opportunity to come on to our terms and conditions of service at the pace they choose. Obviously, you can't replicate everything. If you take the example of outsourced airline staff, we can't continue to give free flights. So we take the common sense approach of equivalents. You can't replicate pensions. We take a common sense approach and try to make it as similar as possible. For example, once we had to break some consultation arrangements because of business confidentiality. So we paid everyone compensation up front on the basis of the maximum an industrial tribunal was likely to have awarded. We don't throw money away. On the other hand, we don't nickel and dime over silly little bits and bobs.'

Dodsworth gives another example of where Cap Gemini cannot be expected to conform to the letter of Tupe law: 'Many employees get a profit-related bonus scheme from their companies. We think it's nonsense for any employee of ours to have an element of their pay dependent on an organization they no longer work for.' To get around the problem, Cap Gemini takes a three-year average of the value of the bonus and pays that to the individuals concerned.

Of 3,500 people who have joined Cap Gemini over the years, bringing with them the former terms and conditions of employment, only 160 still retain non-standard terms and conditions. Those 160, from twelve former employers, have chosen to retain their former employment conditions. They are mostly from the public sector, where people could jeopardise valuable pension rights to which they may have been contributing for many years. Adds Dodsworth: 'We tell most people we would obviously like them to move to our terms and conditions. At any time of their choosing, they are free to come along and ask what the equivalent Cap Gemini offer would be. The reason I like them to take their time and to do the asking rather than the other way around is that in my view they won't do it until they trust us and you have to earn trust. It can't happen on day one.'

In some rare cases, outsourced people insist on retaining their former employment conditions long after the company they originated with has disappeared from the scene. A former Plessey man clung on to his former employment conditions long after the electronics company had been swallowed up by a GEC take-over, but was finally persuaded that sticking to the conditions of a phantom organization did not make a lot of sense.

Often it doesn't take a lot of persuasion to get employees to make the switch to Cap Gemini's standard employment terms. Of the nineteen people who joined Cap Gemini in 1998 under an insurance company outsourcing deal, eighteen chose to sign over to Cap Gemini's terms and conditions of employment from the outset. 'That was a rush of enthusiasm from them. It wasn't us going around twisting their arm,' insists Dodsworth.

Whether or not outsourced personnel switch to Cap Gemini's employment conditions, there is no discrimination between outsourced and recruited staff, according to Dodsworth. 'As far as we are concerned, outsourced people are as much genuine employees of Cap Gemini as recruited people. They're not second-class citizens,' he insists. 'They're not treated any differently. They have the same career development opportunities as everyone else. To come off the X workload and go and work on the Y workload doesn't mean you have to come across to our terms and conditions. The only thing we insist on is that when it comes to promotion, the contract will be offered at Cap Gemini's standard terms.'

Cap Gemini's softly, softly approach seems to have paid dividends. Perhaps surprisingly, the turnover among the people who have joined Cap Gemini through outsourcing is half that of those who were directly recruited. Dodsworth puts it down to the enormous care Cap Gemini takes to ensure the transition periods are as painless as possible. The road show presentations, the one-to-one counselling and the willingness to accommodate to individuals' career aspirations are all part of the package. Another aspect is undoubtedly the fact that outsourced people have the option to carry on doing the job they are familiar with, whereas if they apply for a new job somewhere else there is an element of the unknown. In other words, better the devil you know.

The hurdle of re-location

The biggest hurdle to overcome, in Dodsworth's view, is that of re-location. 'People are a lot more tied to where they work than you might imagine,' he says. In one outsourcing project that involved people moving little more than thirty miles from Telford to new offices at Birmingham, half the workforce opted to look for another job.

Cap Gemini tries to alleviate this problem by establishing offices regionally close to where its main outsourcing deals have taken place. 'Almost all our real estate and all our locations have developed out of outsourcing deals,' says Ingram. 'We created a

Scottish location in Glasgow from a deal with a leading bank; we created our Bristol location from a major tobacco company deal and we are creating a South Wales, Corby and Scunthorpe presence from British Steel. Our Rotherham location is only because of British Steel, but it now has dozens of customers. We tend to use a deal as seed-corn for further development.'

Sometimes the problem has to be solved in another way. Adds Dodsworth: 'There's a deal we are working on at the moment where the company concerned decided to outsource its main frame responsibilities, but it also had alternative jobs for all the people who were currently doing that particular work. Again, this was potentially a location problem, so the company told the employees that legally they could go to us with the workload if they wished. On the other hand, there were still plenty of jobs available for them at the company itself and they all decided to stay. So our people took over the workload.'

Case Study 1 – Ray Murrell

When Ray Murrell and his colleagues heard in 1988 that Plessey was planning to take over Hoskyns (now Cap Gemini), the computer services company, they rejoiced at the idea. They were working at Plessey's central computer centre in Surrey and were already doing a small amount of facilities management (now called outsourcing) and saw it as an excellent opportunity to extend this external work, broaden their horizons and contribute more to the electronics company's profits. Their enthusiasm turned to gloom, however, when they discovered that what Plessey (since absorbed by GEC) actually intended to do was virtually a reverse take-over. It decided to keep Hoskyns as a separate operation and outsource all Plessey's IT operations. Instead of Plessey management running the IT operations, it would be the other way around.

As it turned out, the outsourcing move did Murrell absolutely no harm. Quite the contrary. He is now running Cap Gemini's outsourcing operations for the whole of the UK and his career has progressed in leaps and bounds. However, looking back on that fateful October in 1988 when he was a computer services manager for Plessey, he recalls that his emotions underwent a roller-coaster ride. First, there was the prospect of being in the forefront of an expanding facilities management operation – and then the news that it would be completely the other way around. 'Initially, we saw it as an opportunity to really develop the facilities management side of the business. It clearly gave us the chance to throw off some of the corporate shackles and go forward,' he recalls. 'The first announcement was on a Friday. The following Monday we were told we were all going to be working for Hoskyns, which wasn't what we were expecting would happen.'

The deal involved 348 IT staff, the second largest outsourcing operation that Hoskyns had ever undertaken at the time. The immediate reaction among the Plessey IT people was inevitably negative. Adds Murrell: 'I suppose it was fear of the unknown and realizing we faced a totally different type of company culture.' Some predictable thoughts were going through Murrell's mind: 'If I had wanted to go and work for Hoskyns, I would have applied to the company in the first place. If Hoskyns had wanted me, it would have tried to recruit me. Here I was being forced upon them and you start to wonder how long it will last.'

Murrell had the security of Tupe and the knowledge that he would be entitled to virtually identical terms and conditions of employment, but back in 1988 this was not explained to transferring employees with such care and attention as Cap Gemini ensures nowadays, with in-depth discussions and road show presentations. 'Today we really make an effort to reassure people that we understand all the vagaries of their terms and conditions and how we are going to handle those,' says Murrell. 'The other difference nowadays is that people tend to know earlier that this is going to happen. We often do the road shows now before the deal is even signed.'

In those days, the transfer process was somewhat less structured. A number of senior Hoskyns managers visited the Plessey site to reassure the people being transferred. They were told that once Hoskyns fully understood their aspirations, opportunities would be provided for them to develop their careers. Practically everyone agreed to be transferred and after the reassurances, Murrell estimates that around 80 per cent of them were optimistic that it could prove to be a good move: 'A shock yes, but it could be interesting, because this is what we had wanted to do for some time. We won't have control, but this gives us an opportunity to expand our field career knowledge.'

IT staff from a number of Plessey sites around the country were involved in the deal, but the optimism was strongest among those in the central computer services department. They had already experienced commercial activity in undertaking a small amount of facilities management and they could visualize the prospects for this being enhanced. There was less enthusiasm among some of the IT engineers working at other sites. 'Really, they were engineers working for Plessey who just happened to be given responsibility for IT. Their real *raison d'être* was to be an engineer in a big engineering company. They were probably more concerned about the impact the change would have on them and their careers,' explains Murrell.

Leap into the unknown

The move was also a leap into the unknown for Murrell. Although his work with Plessey had involved him in a small amount of facilities management, it largely concerned deals that had fortuitously come Plessey's way rather than as a result of actively seeking this kind of work. Consequently, he was unfamiliar with the outsourcing market in general and with Hoskyns in particular, even though it was one of the UK's largest computer services suppliers.

This caused him to ponder over the weekend about the wisdom of accepting a transfer deal, but by the Monday morning he had made up his mind to give it a six months' trial. Back then, the employment market for IT specialists was buoyant, as it is today. Murrell was confident that if things did not work out for him he would have little difficulty in finding alternative employment. He thought that would give him enough time to test out Hoskyns' company culture and to make up his mind whether it was the right environment for him. In fact, it only took him three weeks to decide to sign over to Hoskyns' terms and conditions of employment.

What persuaded him to make such a swift decision? 'They were nice people for a start. Everything they said was positive about going forward and they kept focusing on where I wanted to go. They said: "You've been in this in-house operation for several years now and you are obviously comfortable in that, but given the opportunity, what would you really like to do?" In fact, the director I was talking to asked me to give him a list of the things I *didn't* want to do because it would be a lot easier.'

One of the few things Murrell said he would prefer not to do was to work in London, but six months later an opportunity came up for him to work there that was too good to turn down. 'It was the chance to run a profit centre, which I had never done before,' recalls Murrell. 'I had run a cost centre on an in-house basis, but this was a chance to have responsibility for revenue and profits. I thought it would be good for me commercially. Hoskyns said they wanted someone with my background for the job and that it would be an ideal opportunity to see the bigger world.'

It was Hoskyns' policy to replace management in an outsourcing deal as soon as was practicable, to make a quick transition to the Hoskyns' pattern of operating and culture. Ideally, Murrell would have been moved on earlier than six months, but he felt that it would have been disloyal to the Plessey team he had worked with for seventeen years to disappear from the scene too hastily. 'I knew the people very well, we were a very close-knit team and to make that sort of change too quickly would have been too disruptive,' he insists. 'I asked to stay and help go through all the issues about terms and conditions of employment and contractual factors. Such issues as the different way Hoskyns looked at shift work. I was quite keen to see all that through and Hoskyns was happy to let me do all that.'

With these issues taken care of, Murrell jumped at the chance to run a profit centre, even if it meant working in London. It was a regional data centre with a turnover of around £3 million, a fairly modest profit centre in Hoskyns' terms. After a year in London he was invited to take over the running of a larger regional centre in the south of England (with a turnover of around £12 million), where he was able to focus more on the service delivery side of the business. Eighteen months later he returned to London to run all Hoskyns' data centres in the UK. Within another eighteen months Murrell's rapid rise had taken him to one of the summits of opportunity at Cap Gemini – the opportunity to run all the company's outsourcing operations in the UK.'

Looking back on his dizzy climb to the top, Murrell describes what happened to him in somewhat down-to-earth language. 'I suppose Hoskyns gave me a kick in the pants. It just opened up opportunities. To be fair, I had always been happy working at Plessey. I had seen the place grow from a single computer when I started as a trainee operator right through to having about eighteen systems by the time I had become computer services manager. It was a good safe job, a nice team. I had been more than comfortable there. Hoskyns made me realize I was capable of more and they gave me the opportunities to fulfil that potential. It has worked out extremely well for me.'

Growing confidence

Murrell's confidence grew with each new promotion. He admits that he approached his first assignment of running the London profit centre with a certain amount of trepidation, but his fears were soon allayed when he found that promised support from divisional directors was forthcoming. He believes that the

mentoring scheme Cap Gemini has adopted is very instrumental
in helping new arrivals cope with stiff challenges that might at
first seem daunting through lack of experience. 'The mentor is
not necessarily someone who is responsible for you in the line,
but someone with whom you can just talk over issues, worries
and concerns. There was always someone I could ring up to
discuss issues I had never come across before.'

The mentor often gives guidance on the best person to contact
in the company to solve a particular problem. This approach is
reinforced by the induction process Cap Gemini has developed.
Each new arrival is advised about the fifteen or so people he or
she needs to contact in the company to establish a support
network. These are people who head the various divisions and
functions in the company, who all practise Cap Gemini's open-
door policy. It is incumbent on the new arrival to take the
initiative and make the first moves – to telephone these high level
executives, and book time in their diaries to discuss with them
their role in the company and how they can provide support at
times of difficulty. 'It means that when someone finds himself or
herself in difficult circumstances they know who it is they need
to talk to and they can make the network work for them. Let's
face it, that's how things often happen in most businesses,' points
out Murrell. 'That's very much part of the culture of the group –
go and meet these people, network with them, understand who
can help you. The policy is very much that. Whenever senior
managers visit a site they are available to anyone who wants to
talk to them. No one ever says they don't have the time.'

Having himself been outsourced to Hoskyns, Murrell is in an
ideal position to understand the fears and concerns of people who
transfer to Cap Gemini. As head of the outsourcing division, he
is very sensitive to the state of shock many people are left in when
they are unexpectedly faced with transferring to an unfamiliar
organization. He is constantly making adjustments to the road
shows and to the induction policies in the light of lessons learned.

He is aware, for example, that public sector employees are

usually the hardest hit psychologically by an outsourcing deal. This is often because they are more aligned to the Civil Service than they are to the particular job they are fulfilling. They often have strong views about not wishing to work for a profit-making organization. Murrell cites the example of a group of fifty-two civil servants who were being outsourced. There were three contenders at the initial stages of the negotiations – an in-house bid, which was never likely to succeed, Hoskyns and a rival IT services company. The civil servants made it very plain that Hoskyns was the company it would least like to see win the bid.

Some time after Hoskyns had in fact won the deal and the dust had settled, Murrell tried to find out why the civil servants had been so hostile in their attitude to his company. It transpired that the presentation the rival bidder had made to the people about to be outsourced was much more attuned to their needs and concerns. Hoskyns' presentation was fronted by senior line managers who talked about how successful and dynamic the company was and how bright its future. This left the audience feeling that all it was trying to do was sell shares. The rival bidder, on the other hand, put up its HR manager who talked about career opportunities and people management. 'I think that was a lesson to learn,' says Murrell, who ever since has made sure that the road shows include an HR manager.

Case Study 2 – Alan Docherty

The first action Alan Docherty and his computer centre colleagues at a regional health authority took, when they heard rumours in the summer of 1995 that their department was about to be outsourced, was to join a union and demand to be consulted on every move. Docherty was elected union representative. As part of the consultation process he and his colleagues were informed about the shortlist of bidders for the outsourcing contract. Among them was Hoskyns. A vote among the IT team members revealed that Hoskyns was bottom of the list of their preferred bidders. 'There was a lot of fear about Hoskyns,'

Docherty recalls. 'We were certainly very worried. There was a feeling that we were going to be taken on for a short time and then dumped.'

As it turned out, such fears were totally unfounded and Docherty, who is still working for Cap Gemini (which later acquired Hoskyns), is testament to the fact that outsourcing is more likely to bring a new lease of life to someone's career than bring it to an abrupt halt. Many of those who transferred with Docherty at the time of the outsourcing deal have since been outsourced again to an IT services provider that specializes in health care clients. Docherty, however, has seen his career blossom outside health care.

Right from the first moment of hearing that Hoskyns had won the day, Docherty decided to make the best of things. 'There was obviously frustration. I actually took a pay cut to join the health service. It made me happy to think I was doing a bit of good and that nobody was making a profit out of me. There were other people who felt the same way about not wanting to work for a profit-making organization, but it was one of those things you have to accept. We weren't happy about it, but there wasn't much we could do.'

Physically, the transfer did not involve much of an upheaval. Docherty and his colleagues moved to new offices that were only about five miles from their original base. Within nine months Docherty felt comfortable enough under the new ownership to sign over to Hoskyns' terms and conditions of employment. 'My main concern had been that we would be taken on board and half of us sacked within a year. Everything they said implied that wouldn't happen and after about nine months I had made up my mind that I was happy to believe everything they had said in terms of my job security.' A large proportion of Docherty's former colleagues did not sign over and when most of these were later outsourced again to a specialist health care provider, many of them were still on the original health authority terms and conditions.

Staying behind with Hoskyns, Docherty was eventually able to break free from pure health care work and branch out into assignments involving financial, industrial and supermarket chain clients. Initially, however, he was made supervisor of two outsourced regional health authority IT shifts. He enjoyed the increased responsibility, since the workload in his former regional health authority post had been diminishing and he was finding himself far from stretched. Now he can be appointed to any new assignment that comes up. When Cap Gemini wins a new client, Docherty is likely to be involved in reviewing the computer operations and helping to supervise the process of switching them over to Cap Gemini's procedures and standards. In contrast, his first major assignment for Cap Gemini involved computer tracking and monitoring of membership applications for a private health care insurance company.

That, in fact, was the last time Docherty had anything to do with health care. All his projects since have been in other fields. That's how he likes it. 'I've changed my approach. When I came to this company I felt I had to give it my best shot. There was no point in sitting around and thinking how good it all was in the health service. It was a case of getting on and looking after myself, if you like.'

He is confident the future holds good prospects. 'I like the Cap Gemini attitude to promotion. You're not in dead man's shoes. Whatever role you're doing you get promoted to new grades according to how well you're performing. There's a much greater variety of work. I'm always doing different projects and I am quite happy to go on operating that way for the rest of my career.'

One recent project has involved helping a major supermarket chain to prepare for the so-called millennium time bomb that threatens to shut down anything controlled by a computer in the year 2000. Cap Gemini has made him operations co-ordinator for the year 2000, and as the deadline draws closer he expects to be working flat out to avert disaster for several of Cap Gemini's clients.

Docherty is probably a classical example of someone who was almost totally opposed to being outsourced, doing a complete U-turn after the initial shock and turning the opportunity to his advantage. As such, he is a popular choice when Cap Gemini conducts road shows to win over the hearts of newly-outsourced employees. 'They like me to mention the fact that I was a union representative and the fact that I was extremely negative. I just tell people the truth. I'm now Cap Gemini through and through, I suppose, but I wouldn't tell them anything to try to convince them. I just tell them how it is and leave them to make up their own minds. For myself, I'm doing very well, thank you.'

Case Study 3 – Angela Graham-Leigh

Angela Graham-Leigh is one of those rare people who welcomed the prospect of being outsourced with open arms. She had spent most of her career working in the insurance business and was looking for a new challenge, but at the age of forty her chances of breaking into a new career at senior level were pretty slim. So when she heard that her insurance company was planning to outsource part of its IT operations to Hoskyns, she saw it as the answer to a prayer. 'I saw it as my chance to get out of insurance and do something else,' she recalls.

Ironically, her first assignment after being outsourced in 1992 was consulting work for a household name insurance company! It was converting to a new computer system and Graham-Leigh was assigned to advise on questions of data integrity.

Because she welcomed the idea, Graham-Leigh's transfer to Hoskyns went very smoothly. The insurance company that had been employing her had hoped to keep the planned deal a secret to the last moment, but word got out on the grapevine. People from Hoskyns and other potential suppliers were seen visiting the insurance company's IT director and the game was up. 'Rumours were flying around and I think the decision had to be made more quickly than originally planned,' she recalls. 'We had a very early pitch from Hoskyns to say that the final contracts hadn't yet been signed, but this is what is likely to happen to us. So there was some time for everyone to get used to the idea.'

The terms and conditions of employment were pretty much the same in both companies, but Hoskyns topped up Graham-Leigh's salary and that of her colleagues by £1,000 to compensate for loss of some benefits it was unable to maintain. For example, it was not able to offer staff discounts on insurance policies. The former insurance company employees had expected a slightly higher figure by way of compensation. Graham-Leigh switched to new terms of employment in two phases. In the first instance, Hoskyns matched her former employment conditions, but these equivalent conditions were not Hoskyns' standard terms and conditions. However, because she was totally committed to joining Hoskyns, she signed up for the computer company's standard terms within a month.

Tupe does not cover pensions, but Graham-Leigh came to an amicable arrangement with Hoskyns over this as well. At the insurance company she had held a personal pension, to which the company had contributed. Hoskyns was unable to maintain payments on the personal pension, so she left this paid up and joined Hoskyns' company pension scheme.

Breaking new ground
Graham-Leigh wasted no time in letting Hoskyns' management know that she was ready to tackle new assignments, particularly if it would take her away from insurance. She had spent a week at Hoskyns' head office in London becoming familiar with the company's culture and practices when the consulting project was offered. Although it was still to do with insurance, it was very different in nature to the routine work that Graham-Leigh had been so anxious to eschew. 'I had been managing a support team before so I had staff responsibility. This time I was working as a sole representative of Hoskyns as part of a team, but without staff

responsibilities. It was quite refreshing. It was nice to be able to use fields of knowledge that I had acquired in a completely different context.'

She admits, however, that she felt a bit out on a limb representing Hoskyns at a client firm before she had really got to know a lot about the service provider: 'But I had regular contact with people back at Hoskyns' base office. To a certain extent I had to make the effort to go to group meetings to make sure my face was known and to make sure that I got to know a wider set of people.'

After the consulting project Graham-Leigh finally shook off her connections with the insurance industry and was asked to undertake a counselling assignment for a public sector client. She was involved in helping some 100 people, who were being outsourced from the public sector, through the transition phase. 'The experience of having been outsourced yourself is always useful in those sort of circumstances because people relate much more to someone who has been through it rather than just talking about the theory – someone who can actually say they know how it feels. Even though everyone's reaction to outsourcing is slightly different, not many people are going to be as positive as I was about the situation, but I was aware of how some of my former insurance company colleagues felt, a lot of whom were ambivalent about it. Some of them resigned rather than join Hoskyns.'

Graham-Leigh's positive experience also makes her a strong candidate for the Cap Gemini road shows. 'People need a lot of reassuring. Outsourcing comes as a shock. People need to get used to the idea that somebody else is taking over their career paths. Even if they don't want a career and just want to do the same job year after year, that's their choice. Suddenly this catalyst occurs and there is going to be a change.'

As was the case with Alan Docherty, people can often go through a remarkable reversal of attitude once they have recovered from the initial shock. Graham-Leigh recalls that when she was counselling on the public sector deal she was 'castigated' by one person for representing a profit-making organization. 'This chap was saying that he joined the Civil Service because he did not want to work for a profit-making organization. His view was that profit is evil. But interestingly he is still with Cap Gemini. That was back in 1994. Four years later he is still around.'

'Cap Gemini's culture is very good at assimilating all sorts of different people. People who have been outsourced aren't labelled as different from anybody else. Promotion is not normally for a specific vacancy. You get promoted because you're good at what you're doing and have the potential to do more. You can be promoted without any change in role at all. Everything is done on merit.'

In Graham-Leigh's experience, every effort is made at Cap Gemini to ensure outsourced personnel reach their full potential. 'We have full-time resource managers whose job it is to ensure that the right people have the right assignments and that they're matched in terms of skills and aspirations. Some assignments never get advertised. Sometimes people just happen to be in the right place at the right time and they hear about something that is coming up and they put themselves forward. Or one of the managers spots someone's potential.'

There certainly seems to have been no shortage of new opportunities for Graham-Leigh. After the counselling assignment, she became a service delivery manager for an outsourced project at a financial services company, where she managed an IT team based on the client's site. Her latest job sees her in a sales support role. She is now a senior manager in information services management. It is a role that requires her to practise mediating skills. 'It sits between delivery and sales. We go and visit prospects with our sales people. We talk to the prospective client, write proposals and cost deals. We have to make sure that what is being sold we can actually deliver. We are piggy in the middle. We try to keep both sides happy.'

Graham-Leigh clearly relishes the challenge of switching roles, tackling very different assignments and practising new skills. It is in strict contrast to the monotony of her former insurance company work. She is not the least bit nervous about the possibility of the pendulum swinging in the opposite direction – that she might become jack-of-all trades, master-of-none: 'In a company like Cap Gemini I don't think that is likely to happen. I think a wide range of experience is valuable.'

Excellent HR management

Robert Ingram of Cap Gemini believes that the secret of a successful outsourcing contract is bound up in the way the transfer of the people caught up in the transaction is handled. 'Our HR goal,' he says, 'is competitive advantage through the excellent development of people and through the excellent management of the human resource. That's about managing people as individuals, so that each individual feels good about working in this company because there's a future here. Managing the HR is all about being able to construct teams and deploy them fast and furiously with the right skills for the customer.

'Everyone has a one-to-one interview when they join us in order to bring out anything that is of concern to them or any ambitions they have. It might simply be: "I've got a sick mother and I have to leave early on a Thursday," through to: "I'm not very well and I may not be able to work much longer," or even: "I want to be MD of your company – how can I do it?"'

Proactive action

Not everyone reacts passively to the accelerating fashion of outsourcing, however. Steve Floyd, a visiting professor at Cranfield University School of Management, cites the example of someone who took proactive action when outsourcing loomed. In an article in the 15 June, 1997 issue of the *Sunday Times*, written by Margaret Coles, about the plight of middle managers facing the threat of downsizing and outsourcing,

Professor Floyd refers to someone who was running a print shop in a large insurance company in the US.

'He proposed to top management that the business should be outsourced and persuaded them to provide the capital to spin it off. He was left with the print business to run as part-owner and then offered the service to others and became one of Connecticut's leading printers. He took risks. He volunteered to put his unit on the block – but that's better than putting your head in the sand, which is what most people do,' says Professor Floyd.

He advises middle managers who want to stay put to think about how they fit into the company's perception of its core activities. 'If you can show how your unit adds value for the customer, that begins to make it a core activity, a function of what makes the company unique. This sort of thinking positions you to have those conversations about strategy, and to mitigate the risks.'

PULLING OUTSOURCING BACK IN-HOUSE

If being transferred to an unfamiliar organization under an outsourcing agreement is a traumatic experience for many employees, they must greet being transferred back again to their original employers with mixed feelings. Those who were less than happy with working in the alien climate of another organization will probably welcome the chance to return to the fold. Others, however, who may have settled in happily at the new organization and found it conducive to career opportunities and advancement may well find the reversal more than just a little disruptive.

Just such a situation arose at the beginning of 1998 when Sears, the struggling retailing group, announced that it planned to demerge both the Selfridges department store operation and

Freemans, the mail order company, at a cost of £40 million. The write-off resulting from the restructuring included the £25 million cost of outsourcing the group's IT technology and payroll services to Andersen Consulting. The demerger obliged Sears to unwind a £340 million IT contract it had signed with Andersen Consulting only two years earlier. It was announced that the 650 staff involved in the outsourcing would return to Sears, which pledged to find jobs for all of them.

Returning to the fold

Whitbread Beer Company has pulled back in-house about £40 million worth of business from third-party logistics service providers, which has contributed significantly to a 15 per cent reduction in unit costs. The company's distribution is now being run by a central in-house service, which treats each of the business units as a customer. The in-house operation is regularly benchmarked against external providers for efficiency and cost-effectiveness.

John Hartshorne, Whitbread Beer Company's logistics director, points out that all the company's departments and divisions are treated as individual customers with separate service contracts and individual contract prices related to the level of service required. By benchmarking against third-party operators, staff at Whitbread have 'a greater level of commitment to succeed as a commercial business'.

Hartshorne adds: 'The bottom line for our staff is that they have all been briefed that Whitbread will only continue to own and operate its own logistics as long as it continues to provide better service at a lower cost than is available from the competition.'

9
The Virtual Organization – Myth or Reality?

According to a report by Andersen Consulting, *Vision 2010: Designing Tomorrow's Organization*, companies expect outsourcing to increase in importance, pointing towards the arrival of the virtual organization. Forty per cent of survey respondents predicted that their firms would be substantial or fully-fledged virtual corporations by 2010.

Views on whether the virtual organization will ever happen, and if so, when, vary enormously, but most experts agree that the number of functions that companies are likely to outsource in the future will grow steadily and that the functions that continue to be run at the heart of organizations will shrink radically. Bureaucracy will give way to tightly-run core operations where only the activities most critical to the future of an organization are controlled from the centre.

In an article in the *Daily Telegraph* supplement on outsourcing, Peter Pallot observes that high taxes and office overheads incurred in directly employing staff have hastened the advent of the virtual organization. Such bodies, points out Pallot, farm out every function possible, from invoicing and debt collection to core activities performed by casual staff working from home who are called upon when needed.

Simon Wayne, a director of IT consultants Cap Gemini, describes the virtual organization as having undetectable staff. 'If you want to see them, they don't exist,' he says. Most of the people going through the front door of a company work for someone else, suggests Pallot. 'Or they work in other offices miles away. Or from home. Jobs which can be done without going to the office include design of items from clothing to cars to home furnishings, administration, advertising, legal work, publishing, accountancy, journalism, telesales, architecture, secretarial work and translation.'

However, Wilf Altman, writing in the 17 April, 1997 issue of *The Times*, observes that the virtual organization which out-sources almost everything is still rare. 'Yet as more companies in both the private and public sectors sub-contract more activities, they may soon find they need better management skills to keep everything on track.'

Mark Otway, a partner in Andersen Consulting, is doubtful about the idea of companies becoming virtual. 'I don't think it will go that far. Outsourcing will provide organizational flexibility. But there won't be a single model for companies in 2010; it will vary by culture and industry.'

Bob Aylott, head of KPMG's outsourcing advisory service, is convinced, however, that the range of functions to be outsourced will continue to grow and that outsourcing will continue to encroach on functions that were once considered to be critical to an organization's survival as people become comfortable with the idea that such functions can be successfully outsourced. 'I have absolutely no doubt. It's based on comfort pushed along by concepts of core and chore towards the virtual organization, looking at the success of people like Richard Branson with Virgin, which is essentially a virtual organization.

'What Branson has done is to choose products and services

which are essentially commodities and therefore in principle can be delivered by anyone. They don't have any particular product distinction. It is only the gift wrapping that essentially differentiates them. The distinction is at the marketing front end. Whether it's banking or perfumes or airlines, the thing that distinguishes it is not where 95 per cent of the cost is. It is the other five per cent and that's what Branson sees as core. He doesn't dismiss the importance of the other things. He simply uses external people in order to achieve them. He has a few people who think the way he thinks and who are essentially marketing entrepreneurs and all the rest is something somebody else can do.'

Aylott observes that the virtual organization is fashionable and is 'one of the things that has pushed along outsourcing as a management concept. My own personal view is that it requires the distinction between core and chore to be clear and permanent and I don't believe it is clear or permanent. Therefore what you need to do is create a structure which may be virtual in a sense, but is a network where you have various organizations with whom you work – and work very closely – and leverage their intellectual capability and their innovation capability, as well as their delivery capability. The outsourcing model is a delivery model rather than a capability or an innovation model.

'Most companies, for all the talk about business processes running across functions, are still organized into pockets of functional activity. All that is happening with outsourcing and the virtual organization is that these functions are being run under a different structure outside the organization of origin.'

Aylott sees no constraint on the number of functions that can be outsourced in this way 'as long as the outside organization is better at it, more professional at it and has wider experience of doing it, which is why you would choose them probably. Then you ought to be able to leverage that. One company I know has chosen a particular partnering organization because it is very strong in the US and it wants to use it as a pipeline for US ideas into Europe, which at a detailed level it could otherwise never get. That's a good example of a partnering model.'

Just a brand name

British Airways is often cited as one of the companies that is destined to become a virtual organization. Press reports of the company's intentions in this direction appear to have been exaggerated, but if it were to happen, BA would become nothing more than a brand name. All the engineering, the reservations system, flight operations – the pilots, crew and provision of on-board meals – would be outsourced. According to Malcolm Brown, author of an article on outsourcing in a 1997 issue of *Management Today*, the intentions of Bob Ayling, BA's chief executive, are somewhat less ambitious than that. Ayling simply suggested that under a restructuring plan to take the airline into the new millennium, BA planned to achieve some of the £1 billion projected savings from a modest amount of outsourcing.

Brown adds: 'Activities such as baggage handling and refuelling would be scrutinized to see whether they were being done as well by BA staff as they would be by outside contractors. If they weren't, sub-contracting would be considered. Some commentators thought Ayling too tentative. He should go for broke, they suggested, and turn BA into a virtual airline, retaining its marketing function but outsourcing everything else up to and including flying the aircraft. The journalists were clearly exaggerating for effect but were nevertheless reflecting the current popular belief that outsourcing (in which companies concentrate on the bits of their business that give them that competitive advantage and farm out the peripheral non-core bits to others) is by and large a good thing.'

Andrew Lorenz and Randeep Ramesh, writing in the 9 October, 1996 issue of the *Sunday Times*, clearly saw BA's intentions as more radical: 'British Airways will announce a blueprint this week for transferring itself into a "virtual airline" before the year 2000. The plan, to be presented to staff and union representatives on Wednesday, will provide for contracting out all its support services in a move that analysts estimate could reduce its directly employed workforce by 30,000. BA's grand design is aimed at ensuring the airline's competitiveness in the 21st century.

'Code-named *Step Change*, the transformation plan envisages that BA may contract out all operations except for key front-line functions. It would employ only pilots and co-pilots, cabin crew, reservations staff and marketing, sales and promotion personnel. Even stand-by flight crew would not be on the payroll. Nor would check-in personnel. All services on BA's Heathrow "ramp" – notably baggage and cargo-handling – would go, as would catering and the engineering arm, which has already been semi-detached from the airline.

'BA may also sub-contract management of some pre-dominantly tourist routes, particularly in Europe, to focus on its core operation of regular year-round travel. BA will aim to lease the aircraft and engines rather than own them.'

The idea of BA as a virtual organization raises a lot of interesting questions, in Aylott's view: 'What is BA? What is core? Is it its reservations system? Is it its slots? You could argue that's the biggest thing, the most valuable asset that it has. Is it its aeroplanes? Is it its staff in the front office? Catering? You don't want the lowest cost food because food is one of the differentiators that distinguishes one airline from another. It's a very small cost, but in relation to people's feeling about the travel experience, it rates extremely highly.'

That is not to say that an outside caterer could not provide a high quality service, but the key issue, in Aylott's view, is what the outsourcer is expecting from the contractor: 'Are you looking for them to provide it at the lowest cost? Or are you looking for them to come forward with innovative ideas about how they can produce different menus that will travel well (and will appeal to passengers' tastes and become one of the reasons they choose your airline above others)? If you ignore that and just say we want the lowest price, you're missing the point because these functions have value that is not clear.'

THE VIRTUAL MANUFACTURER

Denis O'Sullivan of IBM believes that a trend towards virtual manufacturing is already well underway. 'What are the core competencies of a manufacturer of consumer goods?' he asks. 'Is the core competence the design of those products, the marketing or the selling of those products? Anyone can put beans in tins. There's nothing clever about that. And if someone can manufacture it better than you do, why not let them do it? So you then might have a situation where you have a virtual manufacturing company.'

An example is the UK subsidiary of a leading American manufacturer of wax products. It makes a number of its products, but outsources a lot of its production to third-party companies around Europe. 'They design, package and market the products and are responsible for the content, but don't feel they necessarily need to manufacture them,' points out O'Sullivan.

A Canadian company called Mitel, which manufactures electronic components for the telecommunications industry, with a UK subsidiary at Chepstow in the UK, insists that its manufacturing operation has to compete with outside third-party producers.

O'Sullivan predicts that there will eventually be 'an earthquake almost' once the virtual manufacturing concept catches hold and is seen to be a cost-effective way to do business. 'You're going to have a central organization, which may be called customer fulfilment, that will take orders maybe from customers all around the world, integrating the demand and setting the delivery requirements.' The customer fulfilment department then places orders with the manufacturing department and will tell the manufacturing department exactly what it wants and to what schedule. It may go outside the organization to a third-party manufacturer who is more competitive, offers better quality or better delivery times. The internal manufacturing department will have to compete against the third-party rivals. The important point is that the central customer fulfilment department will control who manufactures what and it will be a quite separate organization from the manufacturing department.'

This, in O'Sullivan's view, is a complete turnaround from the old days when the manufacturing department was king and would produce the goods as it saw fit and leave it to others to store and distribute them.

THE BP EXPERIENCE

BP claims that it is already well on the way towards becoming a virtual organization. It has had a virtual team project up and running for a number of years exploring how to virtualize many of the activities performed in-house today. 'The issue,' says John Cross, BP's head of IT, 'is how to grow as a corporation without sustaining the mistakes of the past, which has just been a question of adding numbers and when there is a recession or cutback the people are the first to suffer. The notion of retaining a very powerful core community of professionals who are there both in growth and if there are downturn periods of your life cycle is a much better one.'

Like most senior managers, Cross finds it difficult to predict exactly how far down the virtual reality track BP is likely to go. 'I don't think we will ever take it to the extremes that Nike has, for example. There are things we will continue to run although there is no reason in the long run why we should. For example, our refinery is really a big pot boiling activity. It's an operational thing. For the time being there isn't a service industry out there that would come and take a refinery over and run it for you.'

However, Cross points to numerous other operations that BP

used to handle in-house that have long been passed on to others to run: 'At one time we owned all our own drilling operations. We drilled holes in the ground looking for new oil. Today in Texas there is a thriving drilling operations service market. We don't own drilling engineers any more; we buy them in. We draw up long-range service contracts and they come in and drill for us.

'When someone builds a focused competency on an aspect of your business and because that's the only thing they do they can do it better than you, the logic drives you to put it out. In that respect, maybe the oil industry has had a longer history of it than most. At one time we owned our own ships used for accumulating seismic data about the ocean floor for oil-finding purposes. There was no self-respecting oil company in the 1950s that did not have its own string of ships delivering its own seismic data. Today, no oil company owns such a ship. That happened forty years ago. People think outsourcing is new, but it isn't when you start to examine the history of organizations and what they've done. The term outsourcing is fairly new, but the process isn't.'

Cross believes that the incursion of outsourcing into corporate activities in the progress towards the virtual organization is inexorable. 'A lot of activities that I would define as the back office activities of corporations are frankly not the main primary focus of the business, and I would include some of the HR back office processes, some procurement and logistics. In other words, it is what I call process outsourcing – an entire business process and its associated activity and systems can go out to an organization that's going to provide, in a sense, a turnkey service. It really allows you as an organization to re-focus. We outsourced our global accountancy processes, for example, to Andersen's and Price Waterhouse. We still retain some accountants in BP, but they deliver the really smart stuff, delivering value to BP.

'Interestingly, when BP decided that outsourcing accounting made sense, there wasn't a market. We sat down with Andersen's and suggested that this might be a new market they could create, which they did. Now all the other big accountancy groups are getting into process outsourcing. So from nothing BP actually created a market, something it logically concluded ought to be.'

Cross dismisses the idea that outsourcing is a passing fad. 'I think it is a pretty remorseless process and I think it is a function of the growing competitive nature of the world. We talk about the global village, but it is amazingly competitive at a global level today, and more and more of these businesses are saying that in order to become global we can't afford to retain practices and activities that are not absolutely at the cutting edge of performance.'

Cross reckons that after reviewing 'the rich history of outsourcing, we have probably seen just about every permutation possible', but he still sees impediments blocking the progress towards the virtual organization. He argues that the IT outsourcing market, for example, has been slow to mature and is not delivering the kind of innovation that he would expect. In discussing his disappointment about this with an outsourcing consultant, it was pointed out to Cross that he should not be surprised by this shortcoming: 'The industry has grown so fast in the past five years that all the big players have typically been operating on a compound growth rate of 30 per cent per annum. Why would you want to mature when the pickings are so easy? All the focus is, in fact, on how to handle that mass of growth. There are no new competitive pressures yet in the market to cause the players to consolidate and really get smarter and better. They are happy just to continue with whatever they are doing almost at the same level of performance.'

VIRTUAL RETAILING

Retailing is another area where the virtual concept is likely to change radically the long-standing methods of operation – although O'Sullivan believes that the impact will be more long-term than in the case of manufacturing. However, retailing raises similar questions about the logic of doing things the way they have always been done and whether new technology and the drive for more efficient, cost-effective methods of doing business is likely to turn long-standing supply chain procedures on their head. O'Sullivan believes that asking where retailers add value opens up a whole new ball-game. 'Do retailers really add value by buying something in, marking up the price and selling it on?' he asks. 'Is that where they're really adding value or are they really adding value by providing a place where you can go and do your shopping? That's the real value they provide to manufacturers, wholesalers and suppliers – and, most importantly, to you and me as consumers. So why do they need to buy the products and own them?

'Why does a retailer have to buy and sell the goods? Why doesn't the retailer simply provide a forum for you and me to buy the goods, whether that's in electronic form or it's in a shop in the high street?'

O'Sullivan cites the example of Walmart, one of America's largest retail groups, where the products it sells remain in the ownership of the manufacturer until they reach the check-out point. 'When the product reaches the check-out counter it passes to the ownership of the retailer and then instantly to the ownership of the consumer,' points out O'Sullivan. 'The only reason it passes into the ownership of the retailer at all is to allow it actually to achieve payment. The manufacturers receive all the information in terms of what the demand is and the manufacturers decide what is going into the shops. The retailer has the final say. It can decline a product it doesn't like or feels is taking up too much shelf space, but strictly speaking it no longer buys and sells the products.'

O'Sullivan points out that virtual retailing already exists on a fairly wide scale with mail order and electronic shopping, where you place an order with a company that doesn't actually have any products at all. Payment is often by credit card, making the transaction almost totally virtual. 'That's virtual retailing,' says O'Sullivan, 'and you will be seeing more and more of that. I think you will see it on the high street as well. These are radically different ways of doing business. If it happens on the high street the consumer won't notice the difference. We will still go there for our cheese and butter, pick the products off the same shelves and probably find the same brand names.'

Electronic shopping promises to plunge consumers into an even more futuristic virtual realm. There are already retailers in the US – and to a smaller degree in the UK – where consumers can place their orders over the Internet and have them delivered to home or office within agreed time frames. There are even companies in the US that provide their customers with freezers to be placed in the garage and which send signals back to inform the suppliers when certain foods are running low. The retailer then contacts the customer electronically and asks whether a top-up delivery is required.

Although most experts are cautious about predicting when electronic shopping is likely to take off in a big way (as opposed to business-to-business electronic commerce over the Internet, which is growing rapidly), the convenience that it provides, especially for busy career people is likely to make it increasingly attractive for certain segments of the population. It will require a major shift in consumer attitudes before the idea spreads to the population at large and there is a considerable number of barriers to be overcome. For example, potential users are concerned about the security aspects of making payments over the Internet and revealing other vital information through the transaction. There is also the issue of why people enjoy shopping. For a lot of people it is as much a social experience as it is a purchasing experience. Much of the enjoyment of on-the-spot buying could be expected to be lost when ordering via a PC screen.

Nevertheless experts predict that it is only a matter of time before a critical mass of people start to see the advantages of doing at least part of their shopping over the Internet. The leading UK supermarkets that continue to spend millions of pounds investing in more and more real estate in their battles to outgrow each other may well live to regret such extravagance. Electronic shopping raises serious questions about the need for vast emporiums if a significant number of people decide they would prefer to sit at home and do their shopping electronically. It may well be that electronic shopping catches on in less time than the payback period for the real estate investments.

Cyberspace entrepreneurs are already grasping the potential and are pioneering ways to employ the Internet to their advantage. Paul Sykes made his millions from out-of-town shops and offices. Today, his business focus is on cyberspace, 'building an information highway instead of a tarmac one'. As chairman of Planet Online, the Internet service provider, he is pushing hard to persuade more British companies to trade via the World Wide Web by offering them an all-in-one route to an Internet site.

'With nearly 200 suppliers offering connection to the Web, the Internet services market has become crowded and confusing for the uninitiated,' observes Trevor Bates, in an article in the *Daily Telegraph* supplement on outsourcing. 'Firms which want to use the Internet for buying, selling and as an information tool are increasingly outsourcing their needs to companies like Planet Online, one of the few suppliers focused on corporate users.'

The Leeds company claimed that by May, 1997, 1,500 firms and 35,000 individuals had signed up to use its Internet service. Planet Online won business worth £4 million in its first year. Its clients include four football clubs – Leeds, Leicester, Sheffield Wednesday and West Ham. Fans calling up the clubs' Web pages can buy soccer strips or souvenirs, and will soon be able to choose a match seat and order tickets.

IMPACT OF THE VIRTUAL ORGANIZATION

In what way would the world be changed if the virtual organization became widespread? Would the average person in the street recognize any difference in the service organizations provide? Would there be a lack of accountability, for example? In Aylott's view accountability will always rest with the outsourcer: 'Legally that would remain the same. What should happen is that in product market development terms the world will speed up. Whether it would speed up in terms of short-term problem solving is another matter. That's the danger, that event-handling would not be as good, but strategic change would be more rapid. So at one level customers would have perhaps more difficulty getting their problems fixed. We all have our horror stories about BT or British Gas or whoever it is. I think with poor contracting it could get worse – but there would be benefits from an increasing rate of change of product, although customers probably wouldn't be so conscious of that.'

How soon before the virtual organization becomes the norm rather than the exception is a matter for debate. What is clear, however, is that with the rapid strides being made by modern telecommunications and the growing pressures on companies to become more efficient and competitive, outsourcing is likely to become an ever more attractive tool. Far from being a fad, it is fast becoming one of the most popular ways for organizations to restructure around their core operations and confront the challenges of the new millennium.

Index

abdication of responsibilities 59, 96
accumulated knowledge 131-132
acquisitions 46
activities vs. competencies 33, 34
adaptability of staff 132
agreements, service level 103-106
AKZO Nobel Chemicals 99
alliances
  see also cooperation 17-25
Altman, Wilf (*The Times*) 164
Andersen Consulting 3, 4, 6, 19, 22, 46, 65, 76,
    77,162, 170
approaches to outsourcing
  biting-the-apple (risk assessed) 36-37
  layer-by-layer (cautious) 36
  striptease (radical) 37-39
Aramark 108
Arthur D. Little Consulting 35
Asda 4, 81
Astbury, Mark (Ventura) 33
asymmetry of information 13-14
AT & T 77
attribute definition 71
Ayling, Bob (BA) 166-167
Aylott, Bob (KPMG) 27, 29, 46-48, 94, 96,
    103-104, 96-97, 135, 137, 164-165, 175

Baldock, Bob (Andersen Consulting) 65
banking 64-65
B&Q 89

Barrett, Louise (Société General) 19
barriers (between functional groups) 63
Bates, Trevor (*Daily Telegraph*) 174
BBC Radio 4 41
BBC Wales 109
Bell Atlantic 77
benefits of outsourcing
  cost-saving and expertise in security 87-88
  and counter-claims, in procurement 62-63
  IT outsourcing with BP exploration 120
  list of 130-131
  partnership, the MSX view 52-53
  positive evidence 125-127
  single sourcing with BOC Australia 127-129
Benefits Agency 24-25
Benetton 25
best customer status, criteria for 129-130
best-in-class providers 94
best practice in decision-making 125
Bewes, Nicholas (BOC) 74, 75
Birmingham City Council 76-77
Blue Water Retail Centre 88
BOC experience
  contract length 95
  Distribution Services (BOCDS) 55-58
  evaluating providers with SESPA 106-107,
    126-127
  global competition 49-50
  mechanics of outsourcing 69-75
  objectives in outsourcing 30-32

single sourcing 92-93, 127-129
spectrum of outsourcing provision 14-16
BP Exploration
  contract length 95-96
  evaluation and selection 78-80
  multiple provision 93
  outsourcing IT 59-61
  positive results 118-125
BP Group 88, 169-171
Branson, Richard 38, 164-165
Brinsden, Peter (BOCDS) 56
British Airways 166-168
British Gas 3, 138, 175
British Standards Institution 88
British Steel 138, 144, 147
British Telecom 79-80, 175
Brown, Jim (BBC Wales) 110
Brown, Malcolm (*Management Today*) 18, 33,
    35, 105, 113, 166
Burgess, Paul (Andersen Consulting) 77
Business Guide to EMU, A (Arthur
    Andersen/Treasury Management) 22
business
  metrics 104-105
  process management 138
  process re-engineering 38, 42
  strategists 29
Business Strategy and Procurement, Centre for
    (Birmingham Business School) 125

Cap Gemini 3, 16, 28, 48, 103, 138-160
capital intensiveness 44
Care Services 88
Carlton TV 28
case studies
  see also BOC experience; BP Exploration
  being outsourced
    enthusiastic 156-160
    sceptical 153-156
    wary 147-153
  cheque-clearing (Royal Bank of Scotland)
    64-65
  cleaning in food processing (Coldwater
    Seafoods) 83-85
  information technology (BP Exploration) 60-
    61
  logistics (BOCDS) 55-58
  non-core activities (BOC) 50
  selecting IT providers (BP Exploration) 78-
    80
  selecting logistics providers 81-82
  travel arrangements (BOC) 74-75
Caterpillar 52
caution (in approach to outsourcing) 36
Cellnet 33
central functions 32-35
change, speed of 131
cheque-clearing 64-65

Ciba Specialty Chemicals 23
cleaning outsourcing
  deployment of employees across boundaries
    111
  mechanics of outsourcing 83-85
  monitoring contracts 107-109
  responsibility retained 102
Cleaning & Support Services Association, The
    85
Cleaning Council, British 84
CMG 66
Co-operative Bank 18, 33
co-sourcing 18-19
Coldwater Seafoods 83-84
Coles, Margaret (*Sunday Times*) 20, 160
collaboration see partnership
communication 100
competitive advantage
  creation of lasting 17
  outsourcing a strategy for 29, 33
  procurement of goods providing 62, 64
  response times 107
  and sharing service knowledge 121
  unexploited 37
competitive differentiation, strengths and
    weaknesses 70-71
competitive disadvantage 134
compulsory competitive tendering 3, 4
computer based inspection 108-109
computer compatibility 127
Computer Sciences Corporation 77
Computer Services and Software Association
    135
computer system failure 93
Computer Weekly 4, 93
Concert 79
confidence building 151-153
confidentiality 3, 5, 86
conflict management 119-120, 121, 132
conflict of work conditions 111-112
conflicts of interest 126
Constable, Nick (*Western Morning News*) 100
continuity 16-17
continuous improvement (philosophy of) 30-32
contract definition 81-82, 104, 116
contract length 95-96, 105-106
contract, clarity of terms 102-103, 109-110, 116
control 99, 104, 115-116
Coomber, Ron (Carlton TV) 28
cooperation 46, 82, 94
core activities
  concentration upon 1
  critical functions 28
  defining 5
  differentiating from non-core 27-39
  ring fencing 35
core competency
  BOC 32

Cellnet 33-34
cost-effectiveness 131
Court, Brian (PMMS Consulting) 62
critical functions 2-3, 28
Croot, Jane (*Make or Buy?*) 3, 42-46
Cross, John (BP) 60-61, 78, 95-96, 119-125, 169-171
Crowther, Jeff (Coldwater Seafoods) 83-84
cultural distinctiveness 132
Cunningham, Edmond (PA) 135-136
customer care 33, 34, 37

Daily Telegraph Outsourcing Supplement 6, 7, 46, 53, 55, 64, 77, 114, 136, 163-164, 174
Darwell-Stone, Julian (Symonds Group) 88
Davis, Sir Peter (Prudential) 22
Debell, Carol (*Daily Telegraph*) 53, 55
Devon County Council 66
disadvantages of outsourcing 131-133
distribution see logistics
Docherty, Alan (Cap Gemini) 153-156
document management 51, 96
Dodsworth, Mike (Cap Gemini) 16-17, 28, 48, 103, 139, 141
downsides multiplex 113-114, 121
driving the outsourcing trend
    access to best global practice 48
    administrative preponderance 44
    cost reduction 47
    cost-effectiveness 50
    empire preservation during restructuring 47-48
    fashionability of the virtual organisation 165
    global competition 43, 45, 49
    investment risk reduction 44-45
    profitability 43, 45
    staff management 49
    standardisation of systems 47
DSS 76, 93
duplication of effort 110, 112
DuPont 20-21
DVLC, Swansea 3

economies of scale 130-131
Economist Intelligence Unit 32, 46
EDS (Electronic Data Systems) 3, 4, 5, 64-65, 93
Electronic Data Interchange (EDI) 23
electronic shopping 172-174
engineering programmes 51-52
Euro currency 133-134
European Administration Resources System (EARS) 93
European Union 136
evaluation process 85, 126, 127-128
evolving process 72
examples of outsourcing see case studies
expectation

definition 117
gap analysis 118
shift 102
shortfall 115-116, 132
expiry dates (of contracts) 71
see also contract length

facilities management 24-25, 32-33, 66-68, 88, 109
Facilities Management, The Centre for 24
factoring 34-35
fashion and the virtual organisation 165
fault correction, mutual 71-72
financial activities 47
fixed cost (turned to variable) 48, 53
fleet management 46
flexibility of contract 8
see also contract definition
Floyd, Professor Steve (Cranfield University School of Management) 160
FM2 84
Forum Corporation 20-21
Freemans 161
functions, critical 2-3, 28
future prospects 133-134

GEC 67, 145
Giordano, Richard 58
global competition 49-50, 121
Goldman Sachs 25
Good, Graham (Palace of Westminster) 107-108
Graham-Leigh, Angela (Cap Gemini) 156-160
Granada Food Services 30
Greater London Council 141
Greenbury, Sir Richard (M&S) 58
growth in outsourcing 6, 32, 43-45, 76, 114, 164
guarding contractors 87, 90, 91

Hamilton-Smith, Karen (Andersen Consulting) 19
Hartshorne, John (Whitbread) 162
Harvard Business Review 60, 78, 119
Health & Safety Inspectorate 102
historical perspective 9-10
Holway, Richard 77
Hoskyns (now Cap Gemini) 138-140, 147-159
House of Fraser 89
human resources 30, 160
Hunt, Dr. Michael (AKZO Nobel Chemicals) 99

IBM 4, 28, 35, 53, 77, 80, 115, 168
ICI 76, 77, 133
ICL 67
ideal model (KPMG Outsourcing Advisory Service) 46-47

Impact Project (KPMG) 118
implanted branches 75
in-house provision, reversion to 1-2, 114-115,
    161-162
individual concerns
    advantages-disadvantages 135
    alternatives offered 142
    bonus schemes 144-145
    breaking new ground 157-160
    challenges 137
    disenfranchisement 137
    disruption 144
    doubts 139-140
    experience disseminated 140-141
    fears 142
    hostility 143-144
    opportunities 137-138, 143, 146
    terms and conditions 144-145
information management 15-16
Information Services, Leading Trends in (Deloitte &
    Touche) 114
information technology see IT outsourcing
information, asymmetry of 13-14
Ingram, Robert (Cap Gemini) 144, 160
Initial Foodguard 83-84
Inland Revenue 3, 76, 93
innovation
    centrality of 17-25
    falling short on 115
    framework for 116-118
    improvement by 52
    tackling 122-125
Integral 88
inter-contract management 61
internal politics 47
international exposure 43-44
Isaac, Tony (BOC) 50
IT outsourcing
    agreements 103
    BP Exploration example 59-61
    growth area review 76-78
    hardware and staff 14
    market dimensions 6
    provider experience 48
    relationship continuity 101-102
    and retail distribution 57-58
    security related 88
    staffing boundaries 112
ITnet 77

Jacobi, Dr. Michael (Ciba Geigy/Sandoz) 23-24
joint ventures 46
JP Morgan 77

Kenny, Denis (Price Waterhouse) 61, 62
key (critical) functions 38
key force shaping enterprise 46-50
Kingfisher 33

Koles, Pam (BOC) 74
KPMG 27, 46, 94, 104, 116-117, 164

labour-intensive manual tasks 41-42, 44
Lane, John (Pagoda Consultants) 76
Lardner, Craig (BOC) 14-16, 31-32, 69-70, 95,
    106, 126-127, 129-130
Leading Trends in Information Services (Deloitte &
    Touche) 7
Lefroy, George (Shell) 9-10
legal services outsourcing 49, 69, 72-73
Liddell M.P., Helen 4
link management staff 111-112, 116, 122
Little, John (PA) 20, 113
Littlewoods (Retail) 30
Lloyd, Dr. Chris (Arthur D. Little) 35
logistics outsourcing 53-59, 83, 80-82, 115-116
Logistics, Institute of 53, 115
London Borough of Brent 93
London Transport Museum 58
long-term contracts 78
    see also contract length
Lonsdale, Dr. Chris (Birmingham Business
    School) 125
Lorenz, Andrew (*Sunday Times*) 166

maintenance work 110
Make, or Buy? (Croot, Jane) 3, 42-46
Management Today 18-19, 33, 35, 105, 113, 166
Manning, Andrew (FM2) 84
Manufacturing and Industry, The Foundation
    for 42-43
market research 38
marketing support 51
Marks & Spencer 55-58
maturing (of outsourcing) 46
MCI 80
measurement criteria 69-70
Meredith, Mark (*Daily Telegraph*) 64
mergers 46
Microsoft 35
Middletons Moore & Bevins (MMB) 106-107,
    126
millenium time-bomb 133-134
mirroring standards 129-130
misunderstandings 100-101, 109, 132
Mitel 168
Mitie Group Plc 68
Moller, Peter (Arthur Andersen) 22
Mondial Assistance 34
Morgan, Nuala (*Daily Telegraph*) 6, 46
MORI 61
motivations for outsourcing see driving the
    outsourcing trend
MSX International 51-53
Murrell, Ray (Cap Gemini) 147-153

National Health Service 3, 137

National Insurance 3
National Savings 4, 5
NEC 8, 114
new challenges 133
Nike 20, 41
Nissan 12-13
non-core subsidiaries 2

O'Neill, Des (Aramark) 108-109
O'Sullivan, Denis (IBM) 28, 53-54, 58-59, 80-82, 97, 115-116, 168-169, 171-173
objectives, monitoring progress 96-97, 101-103, 119
office supplies 61
one-stop providers 50-52
openness 12, 132
operational
    delivery 29
    freedom 38
    statistics 123
opportunity
    climate of 123
    seized 157-160
options numerous 92-93
organisational
    flexibility 164
    focus 124
Origin 77
Otway, Mark (Andersen Consulting) 164
outsourcing (briefly described) 2
Outsourcing Management Group 118
Outsourcing the Finance Function (Accountancy Books) 4
over-control 110-112
    see also control

PA Consulting 20, 32, 33
Pagoda Consulting 76
Pallot, Peter (*Daily Telegraph*) 163-164
Parry, Peter (Sterling Management Consultants) 62
partnership
    building a relationship 12
    facilities management 24-25
    marriage like (BOC and M&S) 58-59
    pipelining ideas 165-166
    shift towards flexibility of 114
    therapy 118
Paul Elliot Consultancy 89
payroll processing 32, 66
performance
    appraisal 70
    focus 130
    standards specification 69-70
Perot, H. Ross 93
personal *see* individual
Pinnacle Alliance 77
pitfalls of outsourcing 131-133

Planet Online 174
Plessey (now GEC) 147
PMMS Consultants 62
Polarstream (BOC) 56
premises management 67-68
    see also facilities management
PricewaterhouseCoopers 61, 90, 170
prime provider 94
prioritising opportunities 31
Private Finance Initiative (PFI) 88, 89
private sector developments 3-4
proactivity of providers 115
problem-solving 126
Procter & Gamble 52
procurement 51, 61-64
production
    design 30
    processes 41-42
property management *see* facilities management
providers, one vs. many 78, 93-95
Prudential 22
public sector developments 3, 4-5
Public Services, Tax and Commerce Union 5
purchase function *see* procurement

quality management 109, 123-124
quality of staff 130
questions, unresolved 5-6

RAC 8, 76, 114
Racal 77
radical approach (to outsourcing) 37-39
Railtrack 100-101
Ramesh, Randeep (*Sunday Times*) 166
rationalisation 44, 75
Rayburn, Mark (Coopers & Lybrand) 90
recession (1988-1993) 1-2
redress 105-106
refuse collection 46
relationship
    management 101-103, 117-118
    model matrix (KPMG) 117
response time 106-107, 126
responsibility retained 101-102
restaurant facilities 30
restructuring at BA 166-168
restructuring, corporate 46-47
retailer/supplier relationship 104
reversion to in-house provision 1-2, 114-115, 161-162
Richardson, Harry (EDS) 64
Ring, David (*Daily Telegraph*) 136
risk assessment consultancy 89-91
risk-assessed approach (to outsourcing) 36-37
Rolls-Royce 76
Rosenbluth International 73-75
Royal Bank of Scotland 64-65

Sainsbury's 81
sanctions 105–106
satisfaction measurement 126
satisfaction to dissatisfaction 117
savings on procurement 62–63
scepticism 124
Schweppes 67
Science Applications International Corporation
      79
Sears 161–162
Securicor 90
security consultancy 89–91
Security Industry Inspectorate 87
Security Management Today 88, 89–90
security of information 133
security outsourcing
      analysis and review 85–92
      apprehensions 86–87
      aversion 92
      comprehensiveness of services 91–92
      and confidentiality 3
Security Systems, National Approval Council for
      (NACOSS) 87
Select 109–110
Selfridges 161
Sema Group 79
service delivery definition 122
service level agreements 103–106
SESPA (supplier evaluation, selection and
      performance appraisal) 70–73, 106–107,
      126
setbacks 119
share price performance 113
shared service centres (SSCs) 22–24
Shell 9–10
Siemens 4
simplistic goals 47
single sourcing 127–129, 132–134
Smith, Ken (Workplace Management) 67, 109
Smith, Sharon (*Daily Telegraph*) 7, 77, 114
Société General (SG) 19
specialisation 17–25
specification (of purchase requirements) 11, 71
      see also contract definition
spectrum of outsourcing provision 14–16
Springer, Don (MSX International) 51
staff
      acceptability 110
      adaptability 132
      continuity 127
      implications for 5–6
      proactive action 160–161
      programmes 51
      turnover 146
      undetectable 164
static focus 125
Step Change Transformation Plan (BA) 167

Sterling Management Consultants 62
Storeshield (BOC) 57
strategic
      implementation 6–7
      insourcing 20–22
      outsourcing as tool 37–38, 42, 46–47
      perspective 97
      procurement 63
      sourcing 20
Strategic Sourcing (PA Consulting) 113
Sturges, Stephen (Derriford Systems) 17, 49
success criteria 31–32
The Sunday Times 20, 160, 166
Sunday Times Sharewatch 21–22
supply chain management 12–13, 31, 50, 53–55,
      116
Supply Management 24, 61–62, 67, 75, 76, 83,
      108, 136
surveillance and alarm technology 87
Sykes, Paul (Planet Online) 174
Symonds Facilities Management 24–25, 88
Syncordia 79

tactical delivery 29
targets 96–97, 101–103, 119
Tarka the Otter (Williamson, Henry) 100
technological
      expertise 131
      focus (of IT) 60
      strategy 123
teleworking 42
Tesco 81
Thomas, Martyn (Deloitte & Touche) 114
The Times 4, 5, 164
TNT 32
Total Quality Management 126
training, global 51, 52–54
transactional perspective 11–13
transdepartmental functions 29
transferring outsourced staff
      administrative nightmare avoidance 144–146
      affinity with original employers 141
      appealing for benefit of doubt 139–141
      conserving system knowledge 138–139
      contractual considerations 143–144
      human resource management 160
      proactive action 160–161
      re-location 146–147
      terms and conditions 144–145
      transitional teamwork 141–143
Transhield (BOC) 57
transport planning 81
Transport, Department of 93
transportation and warehousing 54
travel outsourcing 49, 73–76
treasury management 32
Treasury Management International 22
trend (to outsourcing) 3

Trolley, Edward (Forum Corporation) 21
trust 12, 105, 132
Tupe (Transfer of Undertakings (Protection of
    Employment) Regulations 136, 144,
    148
Turnbull, David (UK 200 Group) 99
Tyler, Geoff (*Supply Management/Security
    Management Today*) 24, 67, 76, 83, 88,
    89–90, 108, 136

UK 200 Group Accountants 99
unexploited competitive advantage 37
Unisys 18
University of Plymouth 66
University of Strathclyde 24

value opportunity agenda 124–125
variable cost (gain from fixed) 48, 53
Varley, Peter (*Supply Management*) 74–75
Ventura 33
venturing (into the unknown) 118–122, 149–
    151
vigilance 105
Virgin Direct 8, 20, 114
virtual organisations
    British Airways? 166–168
    British Petroleum (almost) 169–171

impact of growth 174–175
    in manufacturing 168–169
    in retailing 171–174
virtuality 39, 163–175
Vision 2010: Designing Tomorrow's Organisation
    (Andersen Consulting) 76, 114, 163
Voet, David (BOC) 72

Walmart 172
Wang 96
Waples, John (*Sunday Times Sharewatch*) 22
warranty process management 51
Wayne, Simon (Cap Gemini) 164
Webb, Mark (Mondial Assistance) 34
Western Morning News 17, 49, 66, 100
Westminster, Palace of 107–108
Whitbread 162
wholeheartedness in participation 127
wide-ranging nature of strategy 45–46
Winch, Professor Graham (University of
    Plymouth) 17, 49
Workplace Management 67, 109
world-class capabilities 131

Xerox 4